CLASSICAL WORLD
ALL THAT MATTERS

About the author

Alastair J. L. Blanshard is the Paul Eliadis Professor of Classics and Ancient History at the University of Queensland. His doctorate is from the University of Cambridge and he has taught at the universities of Oxford, Reading and Sydney.

Acknowledgements

For a small book, this work has accumulated a large number of debts. I am grateful to both the University of Sydney and the University of Queensland for giving me the time and resources to complete it. The assistance of the Centre for Classical and Near Eastern Studies of Australia (CCANESA) proved invaluable. My colleagues Caillan Davenport and Janette McWilliam helped me immeasurably in reading and advising on the Roman chapters. Finally, and especially, I am forever grateful to Victoria Jennings who commented on the entire manuscript. Without her this book would have been impossible. This book is dedicated to my nieces, Isobel and Josephine, in the hope that one day they might find it more interesting than Peppa Pig.

CLASSICAL WORLD

Alastair J L Blanshard

ALL THAT MATTERS

First published in Great Britain in 2015 by Hodder and Stoughton. An Hachette UK company.

Copyright © Alastair J. L. Blanshard 2015

The right of Alastair J. L. Blanshard to be identified as the Author of the Work has been asserted by him in accordance with the Copyright, Designs and Patents Act 1988.

Database right Hodder & Stoughton (makers)

British Library Cataloguing in Publication Data: a catalogue record for this title is available from the British Library.

ISBN: 9781444177961

eBook ISBN: 9781444177985, 9781444177978

10 9 8 7 6 5 4 3 2 1

The publisher has used its best endeavours to ensure that any website addresses referred to in this book are correct and active at the time of going to press. However, the publisher and the author have no responsibility for the websites and can make no guarantee that a site will remain live or that the content will remain relevant, decent or appropriate.

The publisher has made every effort to mark as such all words which it believes to be trademarks. The publisher should also like to make it clear that the presence of a word in the book, whether marked or unmarked, in no way affects its legal status as a trademark.

Every reasonable effort has been made by the publisher to trace the copyright holders of material in this book. Any errors or omissions should be notified in writing to the publisher, who will endeavour to rectify the situation for any reprints and future editions.

Typeset by Cenveo® Publisher Services.

Printed and bound in Great Britain by CPI Group (UK) Ltd., Croydon, CR0 4YY.

John Murray Learning policy is to use papers that are natural, renewable and recyclable products and made from wood grown in sustainable forests. The logging and manufacturing processes are expected to conform to the environmental regulations of the country of origin.

John Murray Learning
Carmelite House
50 Victoria Embankment
London EC4Y 0DZ
www.hodder.co.uk

Contents

1

Beginnings

*'Now there are cornfields
where Troy once was.'*

Ovid, *Heroides* (1.53)

In the beginning was chaos. Or so the Greek poets claimed. It is an oddly comforting idea. Chaos – nothingness, the void – at least gives you a starting point for your story. You know where to begin. It is literally Ground Zero. It also gives the account a feeling of progress. After all, anything is better than nothing.

For the classical world, finding a beginning is not so easy. There is no one single moment of creation. The classical world emerges slowly into view and it is not a story of unimpeded success. Things go backwards as well as forwards. The roots of the classical world run deep. Traces of human habitation in the Mediterranean go back as far as 40,000 years. The lifestyle of these early inhabitants was often much better than their European neighbours to the north. As early as 20,000 BC we can see the great advantages that living on the shores of the Mediterranean brought for the interchange of goods and ideas. For example, we find at a number of Palaeolithic and Neolithic sites a bustling trade in blades made from obsidian brought some considerable distance from the island of Melos in the Cyclades. This hard volcanic glass produced blades of exceptional sharpness. Even today obsidian scalpels cut better than their steel rivals.

The ability of the Mediterranean Sea to act as the conduit for goods and ideas meant that the revolutions in agriculture and the domestication of plants and animals arrived in Greece from the Near East much earlier than they did in central Europe or Britain. The cultivation of the famous 'Mediterranean triad' of grain, grapes and olives begins not long after we see similar experiments in cultivation in the Near East at around 8,000 BC. It was

▲ Using techniques borrowed from the Near East, Minoan craftsmen were able to produce exquisite works of art. Gold pendant depicting bees. 1800 BC. Heraklion Museum, Greece. (© The Art Archive/Alamy)

this 'networking' of Mediterranean communities that was responsible for the tremendous advancements we see in Greece and later Italy as these cultures were able to take advantage of the more sophisticated civilizations of Egypt, Phoenicia, and Mesopotamia.

The Greeks were also adept at establishing their own internal networks. The palatial system that developed under the Minoan civilization (c. 3500–1100 BC) on the island of Crete unified large numbers of villages and groups under the control of a central authority. These organizations were able to harness agricultural surplus and transform it into highly developed economies that could support elaborate suprastructures: palaces, complex religious and social practices, and large bureaucracies to administer it all.

Visiting palatial sites like Knossos today, it is hard not to be impressed by both the size and sophistication of this culture. The palace is enormous and complex. Tourists are always struck by the beauty of the frescoes adorning the walls. The treasures unearthed here show exquisite workmanship using precious materials such as imported gold and ivory. It is easy to understand why Sir Arthur Evans (1851–1941), who unearthed this site in 1901, thought that he had discovered the palace of King Minos, the most famous mythical king of Crete. Given Minos' association with the Minotaur (the monster was his stepson), the occurrence of bull imagery in the decoration of this labyrinthine palace only seemed to confirm the relationship. Certainly 'Minoan', the name he gave this civilization in honour of the king, has remained.

Evans was not the only archaeologist who thought that he was unearthing the stuff of legend. A few decades earlier, on 30 November 1876, the archaeologist Heinrich Schliemann (1822–90), at the site of Mycenae, claimed to have discovered the tomb of Agamemnon, the leader of the Greek forces at Troy. Handling the gold facemask that once covered a king's face, Schliemann felt a moment of intimate connection: 'I have gazed on the face of Agamemnon', he is reported to have said.

In fact, Schliemann had discovered the tomb, not of Agamemnon, but of one of the important rulers of the

Mycenaean civilization (c. 1600–1200 BC), named after the site Schliemann excavated.

This civilization flourished from c. 1400–1200 BC when it took over from the earlier Minoan civilization as the dominant power in Greece. The Minoan language (Linear A) remains unintelligible to us, but in the 1950s the language of the Mycenaeans (Linear B) was deciphered by Michael Ventris and John Chadwick. Mycenaean texts present a complex stratified society in which a considerable number of subsidiary officials administer large areas under the control of a ruler based in a central palace. Goods and services were centralized in the palace, which functioned as both storehouse and manufacturing centre.

Evidence reveals that the Mycenaeans were well connected with civilizations outside of Greece. Close ties with both Egypt and most of the principal Near Eastern kingdoms are documented. Textiles and high quality metalwork were popular exports. We find Mycenaean gold, silver and bronze work travelling as far as Italy and the Levant.

The Minoan and Mycenaean civilizations establish a formula for how to succeed in the Mediterranean. The ability to control and harness often-precious natural resources needs to be coupled with a facility to take advantage of the networking opportunities that the Mediterranean provides. It was impossible to stand alone. This last point is underlined by the collapse of Mycenaean civilization. At around 1200 BC, we notice the start of the collapse of important palaces. Fires consume large parts of them. Within the space of two generations, a number of sites are abandoned, never to be reoccupied. The central government collapses. Only dim memories of Mycenaean civilization remained in the Greek consciousness to be reworked as decorative ornaments in oral epic poems such as the *Iliad* and *Odyssey*.

The precise cause of the collapse remains debatable. However, what is clear is that this collapse was not happening in isolation. In the same decades as the collapse of the Mycenaean palaces, the Eastern Mediterranean is thrown into a huge turmoil that is felt as far as Sicily and southern Italy. The great Hittite Empire in Asia Minor falls apart. Many of its cities are abandoned or destroyed. Egypt is invaded by mysterious 'sea people' who plunder the kingdom and leave it immeasurably weakened.

The period after the collapse of the Mycenaean civilization used to be known as the 'Dark Ages'. These days we prefer less pejorative terms such as the 'Iron Age'. Certainly life in the 'Dark Ages' was not as bleak as scholars used to think. Yet, it is clear that the turmoil around 1200 BC took its toll. The sundered networks took a long time to recover and substantial reorganization needed to occur in both the Mediterranean and the Near East before either group was ready to engage with each other again on a scale that matched previous exchanges. Yet the formula persisted: as Greece emerged resurgent, the twin principles of internal organization and external engagement are once more recognizable. Politics and diplomacy are the bedrock of any successful state. It is these that keep chaos at bay.

2

Athens – the 'lucky' city

'Our government favours the many instead of the few; this is why it is called a democracy. Our laws afford equal justice to all. Advancement depends not on social standing, but on ability.'

Pericles, Athenian statesman (c. 495–429 BC)

Athens was the city that never was supposed to succeed. It was the runt of the litter. If you had asked a Greek in the sixth century BC which city-state was destined for greatness, he would have named numerous cities ahead of Athens. Sparta by that time had established itself as ruler over large sections of the Peloponnese. Corinth was an impressive commercial capital whose goods could be found all over the Aegean. Miletus on the coast of Asia Minor was not only established as one of the centres for ancient philosophy and science, but was also an important wealthy power, having founded over 90 colonies that spread from the Black Sea, down the coast of Turkey, and out into the Mediterranean. There were dozens of contenders who had a better chance of making it big than Athens.

Yet in the space of a little over 100 years, Athens went from the back of the pack to its undisputed leader. It was a rise that astonished even the Ancients. Writing at the end of the first century AD, the biographer and essayist Plutarch wondered how Athens achieved greatness. Was it luck or cunning? Did Athens deserve to be more famous for her generals or her artists and philosophers? These days we might be surprised to learn that it was her success in military exploits that Plutarch identified as Athens' greatest asset.

For us, Athens is synonymous with the rich life of the mind and the skills of her artisans. It is her cultural products that we admire so much. Her reputation rests on her democratic innovations, the elegance of the Parthenon, the power of her tragedy, and the cleverness of her philosophic schools. Yet all of those marvels, for which she is justly admired, could not have occurred had Athens not also been one of the most effective and ruthless military powers of her age.

Admittedly, Athens enjoyed some natural advantages. It is important to remember that most Greek city-states were tiny. The average Greek city-state occupied a landmass of between 50 and 100 square kilometres and had a population of approximately 400 to 900 male citizens. In contrast, the area of Attica is approximately 2,650 km^2 and during her height Athens had a population of 30,000 male citizens. Along with wives, children, slaves, and foreigners, this gave the city a population of about 300,000.

Indeed, the difficulty of marshalling Athens' resources may explain why the city was such a late developer. The early history of the city is one beset by stories of infighting among regional factions. Greek myth speaks of Attica (the area surrounding Athens) as home to 12 independent cities and, while this overstates the degree of urban sophistication of archaic Attica, it nevertheless correctly captures the level of intense regionalism. The unification of Attica under a central urban authority based in Athens was neither an easy process nor, ultimately, a completely successful one. Even in the fifth century BC, long after the unification of Attica, the historian Thucydides describes the emotional wrench that many Athenians felt as they left their villages in the country and went to cower behind the walls of the city as the opposing forces from Sparta invaded Attica. For many Athenian citizens, their ties with their local region were as, if not more, important than their ties to the city of Athens.

▶ Tyranny

The Athenians liked to pretend it was the mythical King Theseus who unified the region of Attica under the control of Athens. Theseus – who slew the Minotaur and performed numerous amazing tasks including ridding the countryside of dangerous monsters and evil bandits – was Athens' answer to Heracles, and his feats were clearly modelled on his more famous predecessor. On the Athenian treasury at Delphi the sculptural decoration features the labours of Heracles and Theseus side-by-side with the implicit invitation to compare the efforts of the two great heroes. Almost every indigenous institution that the Athenians valued was attributed to Theseus.

In fact, the person who should get the greatest credit for unifying Athens was not a mythical monster slayer, but an ambitious politician by the name of Pisistratus (c. 600–527 BC). His attempts to seize power in Athens dominate the second half of sixth century Athenian history. Our undoubtedly exaggerated accounts stress that there was nothing that Pisistratus would not do to get into power. He faked attacks on himself in order to be awarded a bodyguard. He dressed a woman up as the goddess Athena in an attempt to fool the Athenians into believing that he enjoyed divine favour. Finally, he invaded Attica with the backing of mercenaries in c. 546 BC and established himself as tyrant of Athens for almost 20 years. When he died, he was succeeded briefly by his sons Hippias and Hipparchus.

The reign of the Pisistratids (as they are known) represents an early Golden Age for Athens. The

Pisistratids provided Athens with her first aqueduct, securing a water supply for the city. They encouraged the rural economy by promoting the cultivation of the olive. Under their influence Athenian traders and trade goods travelled as far north as the Black Sea and as far west as France. Pisistratus deserves credit: he made Athens look beyond her borders to seek a role on the Panhellenic stage. He put an end to factional infighting through a combination of exiling, bribing and neutralizing his opponents. He reorganized the city's central marketplace and undertook an extensive building programme. A sign of this regime's ambition can be seen in the enormous temple to Olympian Zeus which the Pisistratids initiated – a structure so large that it was not completed until many centuries later in the reign of the Roman Emperor Hadrian. Today its enormous columns remain one of Athens' most striking landmarks. Under Pisistratus' rule, Athens became a centre for poets, artists and thinkers.

▶ Birth of democracy

Of course, no democratic Athenian would ever admit (at least not in public) that tyranny had its benefits. Pisistratus' name was maligned and his achievements reattributed to other less problematic individuals – the Athenian democracy ensuring that his legacy should remain forever ambivalent.

The overthrow of the Pisistratids came to be regarded as a watershed moment in Athens' history. Their downfall was the result of a combination of factors. Exiled opponents of the regime fermented discontent. Sparta, worried about the rise of Athens, was keen to assist in the removal of the regime. And the regime was weakened when one of the sons, Hipparchus, was assassinated in a homosexual lovers' dispute. A rule that began as relatively mild became increasingly brutal and unpopular. All these factors came to a head in 510 BC and resulted in the overthrow and exile of Hippias. Intriguingly, the overthrow seems to have been a genuinely popular movement rather than one instigated and controlled by members of the elite. The rule of one man gave way to democracy.

The democratization of the city is a trend that we see happening in many places all over the Greek world. Sparta may have retained having two kings until the end of the third century BC, but even by the seventh century BC, their powers were severely curtailed by the citizen population. The Kings may have controlled the agenda, but they needed the ratification of the people before their proposals were put into action. Time and again we see, throughout the Greek world, the establishment of an ever-increasing number of councils and assemblies as franchise was extended beyond a few elites to more and more people.

Athens was unique in perfecting this democratic trend. In the wake of the overthrow of the Pisistratids, her people established the most important and influential democracy in the ancient world – the one by which the term 'democracy' was judged. The centrepiece of the system was the Assembly (Gk. *ekklesia*), an organ that met at least three to four times a month to vote on all matters relating to governance of the State. The Assembly was an institution in which any male citizen (women were excluded) over the age of 20 had a right to vote and speak, and which valued 'frankness of speech' as one of the pre-eminent civic virtues. Attendance was healthy: there were rarely fewer than 6,000 citizens attending, and for important civic matters many more would turn up. Attending the Assembly became almost a form of sport or entertainment. In 427 BC, one frustrated speaker berated his fellow citizens for behaving like spectators who come along just for the thrill of hearing novel arguments.

Magistracies and privileges that had previously been the sole preserve of the elite were now awarded by lot to any eligible male citizen who put his name forward. The Athenians were much keener on awarding political positions by chance than using elections. The only notable magistracy in Athens that was an elected position was the generalship. A lottery was considered much more democratic than election as it provided a level playing field in which differences in wealth, education and background between candidates were entirely erased. It also created a space for the divine to participate in the election. If the lot did not fall your way, it was clearly the will of the Gods.

The Athenians were rightly proud of their democratic experiment. No other state had instituted democracy so widely or so deeply. However, it is easy to be overly romantic about this system. The gap between rich and poor in Athens remained extremely wide and the wealthy still enjoyed tremendous advantages. It is one thing to allow anybody to stand for office, but it is another thing to have the time and resources to feel that you could fulfil the required duties and so put your name forward. Anyone could speak in the Assembly, but it is striking how regularly the same expensively-educated voices seem to be heard.

By transferring power away from the realm of private households into public assemblies, Athenian democracy disadvantaged women who traditionally had wielded greater power within familial structures. Women still had influence in affairs, but it was indirect. For example, a litigant in the Athenian law court warns the jury about facing the wrath of their wives and daughters when they go home, if they get the decision wrong. Female opinion mattered, even if women did not enjoy the power of direct franchise.

These democratic innovations would have remained a curious anomaly were it not for a series of the events that pushed Athens into the spotlight. The event that ensured Athens' greatness was the Persian Wars.

▶ Persian Wars

The Persian Wars provided another opportunity for Athens to confound expectations. Persian expansion in Asia Minor and the surrounding areas had gone largely unchecked for over a century. Their resources and army dwarfed their Greek opponents.

Ambition and fear were Athens' driving motivations in the conflict. It was a desire to play a greater role on the Panhellenic stage that encouraged Athens to provide support to the failed revolt by Greek forces against Persia in 498 BC and so incur the ire of Persia and make conflict between Greece and Persia inevitable. And it was fear that Persia would impose on the city the ousted tyrant Hippias as a sympathetic ruler and destroy democracy that caused Athens to oppose the Persians so strongly when their forces landed in Greece in 490 BC and to defeat them on the plains of Marathon.

Marathon quickly entered into Athenian mythology. In theory, the battle should have been an easy Persian victory. The Athenians were substantially out-numbered. The Persian troops were seasoned veterans. However, through a combination of luck and sound military judgement the Athenians were victorious. Attacking on the run, the Athenians caught the Persians by surprise. Confusion reigned on the battlefield. Large sections of the Persian army, which still had not properly disembarked from the Persian ships, were caught off guard in the muddy terrain and slaughtered. The few Athenians that died in the conflict quickly became regarded as heroes – the epitome of the democratic, freedom-loving citizen defending his homeland. The battle site and the tomb of the Athenians who died there became a site of pilgrimage. Over a century later, as part of their education, all

Athenian young men were required to visit and make offerings to the tomb of the war dead. The myth of Marathon refused to die. Many centuries later, the writer Pausanias records that it was possible at night to hear the ghosts of Greek and Persian warriors still fighting on the plains of Marathon.

These days we remember Marathon for the long running race named after the battle. The event was established at the first modern Olympic Games in Athens in 1896. The distance (c. 40 km) represents the distance between the plain of Marathon and Athens and the event supposedly commemorates the run of the brave Athenian who rushed to Athens to announce the victory over the Persians. He ran the whole distance without stopping. Arriving at the Assembly, he proclaimed the victory and then promptly collapsed and died. The story of the run is told by Plutarch in his essay 'On the Glory of Athens'. In fact, there is good reason to doubt Plutarch's version: he was writing centuries after the events, and it is hard to find any contemporary evidence. The historian Herodotus, our closest contemporary source, does describe an incredible run undertaken by an Athenian, but this run was not to Athens, but to Sparta to seek help. It is this run that seems to have become confused in our accounts. Modern athletes should be glad for the confusion: had the instigators of the modern Olympic Games followed Herodotus instead of Plutarch, athletes would be facing a gruelling run of close to 246 km (the distance between Athens and Sparta).

The following decade was to present even greater opportunities for myth-making. In 480 BC, the Persian King Xerxes returned with an even larger invasion force. Once again a coalition of Greeks stood against him. In this conflict, the battles of Thermopylae, Salamis and Plataea came to join Marathon among the list of definitive moments when Greece demonstrated her superiority against the foreign foe. Different Greek communities, of course, invested different amounts of pride in the various battles. The Spartans, for example, never forgot King Leonidas and his brave 300 Spartans who died, as their epitaph recorded, 'obedient to their laws' at Thermopylae. The Athenians preferred to remember Salamis where, in the straits off the Attic coast, the Athenian navy defeated the Persian forces and dealt the invasion a fatal blow. Those who fought at Plataea sought to commemorate this moment when the remaining land forces were mopped up and the final nail was put in the coffin of Xerxes' ambition.

Remembering and explaining the Greek victory in the Persian Wars became one of the central tasks of subsequent generations. Herodotus practically invented the genre of history to help record 'the great and marvellous deeds of Greeks and foreigners and the reason that they came into conflict'. It was impossible to travel in mainland Greece without being reminded of the Persian Wars. Memorials, shrines and victory monuments dotted the landscape, including the most important sanctuaries of Greece.

▶ The Athenian Empire

Athens, in particular, had a vested interest in perpetuating the memory of the Persian Wars. In the wake of the victory she had managed to transform a large section of the Greek coalition against Persia into her own private fiefdom.

Almost immediately after the battle of Plataea, dissatisfaction from a large number of allies bubbled up against Sparta, the leader of the Greek coalition. Athens was able to harness this opposition and form an alternative political arrangement to the coalition – one where Athens, not Sparta, would be the leader. Known by historians as the 'Delian League', this alliance had three ostensible aims: to exact revenge on Persia for the damage she had inflicted on Greece; to free the remaining Greek cities that were under Persian control; and to protect Greece from further invasion.

In practice, Athens ran this alliance like a protection racket, extorting money from her allies on the pretext of an always imminent Persian threat. Attempts to leave the League were treated brutally. An ally who tried to secede could expect to have the ringleaders of the revolt put to death, the walls of the city pulled down, their armed forces disbanded, a garrison of Athenian soldiers stationed on the ally's land and a pro-Athenian government established. Through her superior navy, Athens was able to enforce her rule throughout the Aegean.

Of course, the Empire was not without its benefits. Piracy, the plague of the Mediterranean, was removed.

Wealthy and talented allies found opportunities and a market for their skills in Athens. In the marketplace of Athens it was possible to find Egyptian perfume sellers, Libyan grain merchants, Phoenician textile workers, and Thracian princes keen on enjoying some sightseeing. Many local elites found it very comfortable to cohabit with this imperial power.

Within Athens, the benefits of empire were distributed widely. Athens became famous for the large and splendid festivals she was able to support, and her monumental building programme. The urban poor found work in the navy as well as enjoying pay to act as jurors in the law court. The rich may have grumbled that there was little for them in the Empire, but in fact many wealthy Athenians were happy to seize the opportunities that the Empire provided, whether it was serving on embassies to foreign courts or the possibilities of overseas landholding.

▶ The Peloponnesian War

Not everyone was pleased with Athenian expansion. Sparta disliked finding herself usurped as the leading state in Greece. Corinth found her commercial and political interests threatened by the Athenian Empire. As Athens continued to press her interests she found herself increasingly stepping on the toes of these powers. Eventually open conflict became inevitable. In 431 BC, the Peloponnesian War broke out between Athens and her allies and Sparta and her allies (the 'Peloponnesian League').

Neither side expected the conflict to last as long as it did or be as wide-ranging as it was. Previous Greek conflicts tended to be resolved within a year. A five-year conflict was regarded as long. The idea of a war that went on for close to three decades was inconceivable. Even the Trojan War, the greatest war in Greek myth, only lasted for ten years.

The reason why the war proved so inconclusive for so long was that Sparta was a land-based power and Athens was sea-based: it was very difficult for one state ever to land a decisive blow on the other. That all changed when Persia entered the conflict. Wooed by both sides, she eventually chose to back Sparta. From that moment, Athens' fate was sealed. Persian wealth allowed Sparta to equip herself with a navy and, after a number of unsuccessful battles, the Spartan fleet was able conclusively to defeat the Athenian navy at the Battle of Aegospotami in 405 BC.

▶ Aftermath

The end of the Peloponnesian War should have been the end of Athens. Certainly a number of Sparta's allies argued for the complete destruction of the city. Sparta chose another path. She dismantled the Empire and democracy and installed a short-lived pro-Spartan government.

In the wake of the Peloponnesian War, we see a number of powers attempt to establish control over all of Greece. Sparta attempted the task first. However, she proved ill-equipped to manage an Empire beyond her traditional area of control in the Peloponnese. Moreover, her imperial actions angered a number of her allies, most notably Thebes, and they worked against her plans. Her final mistake was to get Persia off-side by backing a pretender to the Persian throne. Persia withdrew her support and actively worked to thwart Sparta's interests.

Curiously, we see Athens entering the stage again. Persia assisted in this, but Athens was also aided by a number of her former allies. Indeed, when Athens proposed to restore a version of the Delian League, a number of states were happy to join. Athens promised that she had learned from her mistakes and would not violate the spirit of the agreement of union. This new confederacy was to be a coalition of allies, not a pact between imperial ruler and subject.

Sadly, these noble aims were quickly abandoned and the hopes of the allies turned out to be misplaced. Within a few years, Athens was back to her old ways. The Second Athenian Confederacy proved to be as brutal and imperialist as its predecessor. Athens' disillusioned allies revolted and were ultimately successful in dismantling Athens' power.

Power, however, abhors a vacuum, and new contenders soon emerged to take the place of Athens and Sparta. The first was Thebes. Throughout the fourth century BC, this city had grown in power and status. Athenian plans were continually thwarted by Thebes, and Theban troops defeated the Spartans in a number of important battles, ultimately putting an end to Sparta as a mainland power.

Indeed, were it not for another player, we would regard the fourth century BC as the 'Theban century'. Unfortunately for the Thebans, they found themselves outplayed by one of the greatest politicians and strategists that the Greek world produced, Philip II of Macedon (382–336 BC).

Philip transformed a kingdom on the periphery of the Greek world into a major power. Macedonia had always been significant. Her gold mines and capacity to provide ship-building timber had meant that the Kings of Macedonia were routinely courted by Greek cities. Philip's genius was to consolidate his control over this always fractious kingdom and revolutionize its armed forces. Macedonia became practically unstoppable.

Too late Athens and Thebes recognized the threat that Philip posed. Banding together they opposed him at the Battle of Chaironea (338 BC). Philip inflicted a catastrophic defeat on both forces. Indeed, seeing the bodies of his opponents piled so high, Philip wept for the death of so many brave men.

Chaironea marked the end of one age and the beginning of a new one. Philip, however, would not live to see it: assassinated in 336 BC, his mantle was assumed by his son, Alexander (356–323 BC), whose subsequent exploits in conquering Persia and the surrounding kingdoms would earn him the title 'the Great'.

Historians call this era the Hellenistic period and it is distinguished by a number of new features. Politically, the Battle of Chaironea saw the end of the citizen and the city-state as the dominant political units. There would still be cities, but power now moved to princes and kingdoms. The centre of culture shifted away from mainland Greece to new centres such as Pergamon, Ephesus, Rhodes and Alexandria. These new capitals saw novel forms of Hellenism develop as influences from Egypt and Asia Minor transformed what it meant to be 'Greek'. It was an exotic and exciting world. It is easy to see why so many have been entranced by the romance of Alexander and have been keen to see in him more than just a drunken, adventure-loving bandit with a bloodthirsty, ruthless streak and a taste for booty. For all his many flaws, the fact remains that, after Alexander, the Greek world was never the same.

This new world order faced a number of challenges. Alexander's Empire stretched from mainland Greece through Egypt and Persia to modern-day Pakistan. It covered numerous people and cultures. It was never going to last. Almost immediately on Alexander's death, we see the Empire divided among his ambitious generals. Fresh divisions and kingdoms were created. The most successful were ones that grafted onto pre-existing political units. The general Ptolemy (c. 367–282 BC) took over the kingdom of Egypt and established one of the most stable Hellenistic dynasties, enduring until 30 BC when the last Ptolemaic queen, Cleopatra VII, committed suicide to avoid capture by the Romans. Other Hellenistic dynasties took over parts of the old Persian Empire or based themselves on important Greek cities.

In each case, these new rulers had to adapt to ruling a subject people that were often very culturally distinct from the rulers themselves. They succeeded through a combination of permitting pre-existing arrangements to stand and adapting to local customs to create a new hybrid culture. It is these series of compromises that make the Hellenistic world so vibrant and distinct. It was an extraordinary world in which Greeks could portray themselves as pharaohs or dress as Persians, and Greek influence can be seen from the sands of Egypt to the slopes of the Hindu Kush.

▲ Hellenistic rulers were quick to assimilate local customs. Relief showing Ptolemy II making offerings to Hathor and Isis. Philae Island complex, Egypt. (© National Geographic Image Collection/Alamy)

3

Rome

'Roman ... these are your skills:
to pacify, to impose law,
to be merciful to the conquered,
and to beat down the proud'

Vergil, *Aeneid* (6.1151–54)

▶ Introduction

The Romans never tired of talking about the origins of their state. It was a topic that fascinated them. The problem for us is that it is impossible to reconcile the plethora of stories that they told into one continuous and consistent narrative. This variety of stories is further complicated by the reluctance of the Romans ever to agree unanimously on the 'facts' of their history. Take, for example, the date of the founding of Rome. Traditionally, we like to say that Rome was founded in 753 BC, because we have chosen to endorse one particularly influential ancient scholar, Marcus Terentius Varro (116–27 BC). Throughout the period of the Roman Republic (c. 509–27 BC), the question of the founding date of Rome was much debated. It became a tradition to begin all Roman histories 'from the founding of the city' (Latin: *ab urbe condita*). The problem was that nobody could agree on when precisely that date was. This should make us wary about putting too much weight on these literary accounts.

Nevertheless, while we harbour suspicions about the completeness and accuracy of these early 'histories', they do give us insights into the desires and concerns that these early commentators wanted to communicate. People write history for a reason, because they believe that the past can speak to the present. The themes that emerge from the histories of Rome tell us a lot about how Rome saw herself, how she wanted to be seen, what she wanted, what she feared, and what she hoped for the future.

Moreover, these stories matter because they tell us what makes Rome distinctively Roman. If we look at the archaeological picture of earliest Rome, it is hard to see anything that sets the community of Rome radically apart from neighbouring populations on the Italian peninsula. In terms of their material culture, the way they settle the land, and their social practices, the inhabitants of the Tiber valley look not dissimilar to everybody else. We can spot broad ethnic differences that separate out the various peoples of the Italian peninsula, but isolating a distinctively 'Roman' approach to their everyday lives proves elusive. To understand Roman identity we need to look to stories, not to things.

▶ Early Rome

When Romans tell the story of the earliest part of their history, they do so with two particular outcomes in mind. They want to establish the divine credentials of the city and they want to justify its eventual (Republican) form of government. There is a certain tension between these two aims. Stories about acts of Divine Will normally involve authoritarian figures (Gods, kings, princes, etc.) who wield tremendous powers to achieve marvellous aims. Gods favour heroes not committees. In contrast, Republican government is all about devolved power. It is a form of government that privileges consensus and collegiality. A narrative that seeks to combine these two elements is inevitably going to be complicated.

Formulating any sort of coherent narrative ultimately does violence to the richness of the mythic tradition. However, we misunderstand myth when we expect it to hold a consistent line. For example, the Romans disagree as to who laid out the principal sanctuaries in their city. Sometimes they accord the honour to Romulus or another early king. Sometimes part of the task is awarded to Hercules, who supposedly accomplished it while stopping in Italy on his way back from his labour of capturing the cattle of the monstrous Geryon. When it comes to early Rome, it is better to focus on the narrative function of myth rather than the multiplicity of conflicting details. It is much more rewarding to focus on the big themes.

One of the biggest themes is the idea of divine providence. From the start, it was clear that the Gods wanted Rome to exist. It was destiny. All the myths about early Rome point in this direction. Our two most famous accounts of the founding of Rome – the story of the wandering of Aeneas, and the story of Romulus and Remus – each attest to, and explore, this divine plan.

It is understandable that a new city would seek a glorious past. Rome was no different from many other cities in wanting to embed herself into the mythic fabric of the Mediterranean, and no greater prize existed than claiming a part in the Trojan narrative.

The Roman poet Publius Vergilius Maro – we call him Vergil (or Virgil, following a very late spelling) – gives us the most complete version of how the fates of Troy and Rome are interlinked. His epic poem the *Aeneid*, written under the reign of Emperor Augustus (63 BC–AD 14), sets out how the Trojan prince Aeneas escapes the destruction of Troy and travels with his men to seek sanctuary on the Italian peninsula.

At every step, Aeneas is haunted by his destiny: to help found a great city. Such an important task befits the son of the Goddess Venus. Unlike the children of Gods, the offspring of Goddesses are comparatively rare. They are marked out for great things. It is no coincidence that the greatest of the Greek heroes, Achilles, was the son of the divine Thetis. Aeneas' destiny makes him a target for those divine beings who are jealous of the future greatness of Rome, such as Juno, wife of the principal god Jupiter. Juno does her best to throw Aeneas off track. But the manifest destiny of Rome is not easily thwarted. When Juno attempts to divert Aeneas away from Italy by instigating a love affair between Aeneas and Dido, the Queen of Carthage, the Gods themselves are forced to intervene. Mercury, the messenger god, is dispatched to bring him to his senses and remind him that his fate lies elsewhere. Aeneas answers the call and slips away to do his duty. Distraught, Dido commits suicide, calling down curses on Aeneas as she dies – curses that will come to fruition in the future conflict between Rome and Carthage.

Even from this brief sketch, it is possible to see that the *Aeneid* does a lot of work. It creates a genealogy for Rome among the great cities of the Mediterranean. This aspiration was not confined to Rome alone. Images of Aeneas crop up throughout the Roman Empire; even provincials wanted to share in this 'foundation story'. The *Aeneid* also provides an explanation of, and simplistic justification for, historical events such as the Punic Wars between Rome and Carthage. Yet, seemingly paradoxically, one crucial service that the *Aeneid* does not provide is a narrative of the founding of Rome. When Aeneas arrives in Italy, he is welcomed by the Latini (Latin) tribe living in the Latium region. After fighting off a suitably monstrous rival suitor, Aeneas marries the daughter of Latinus, King of the Latins, and founds not Rome, but a city named after his new wife Lavinia. Eventually, Aeneas dies – in some accounts in battle, in others he just disappears – and is transformed into a divinity. Rome was not even founded by Aeneas' son, Ascanius. He founds the city Alba Longa and it is from the descendants of the line of rulers of Alba Longa that Rome is founded.

Founding a city is a complex business. In the ancient world, cities often arise out of tragic circumstances. The founders of cities are idiosyncratic individuals. They are often marked by physical deformity or unfortunate life stories. They might stutter, limp, be blind, or shunned by their wealthy and royal families. There is always something that marks them out.

Romulus and Remus fit well into this pattern. They were the twin children of Rhea Silvia, the daughter of Numitor, the former King of Alba Longa, who had lost his throne to his usurping younger brother Amulius. Amulius killed Numitor's only son and tried to ensure Rhea Silvia remained childless by making her a Vestal Virgin. Fortunately, fate had other ideas and Rhea Silvia fell pregnant. The father is traditionally Mars, although some accounts award the honour of paternity to Hercules, and others to an anonymous mortal rapist. Fearful of these children, Amulius sought to kill them by exposure and they were thrown into the River Tiber. However, the children were saved by the river God who refused to let them drown, but instead carried them safely to the riverbank where they were suckled by a sympathetic wolf. Subsequently, the infants were found by a passing shepherd who raised them.

Eventually, the twins discovered their true origins, overthrew their great uncle in Alba Longa, and restored their grandfather to his rightful position. Rather than return to Alba Longa, they decided to found a new city. At this point, the unanimity that had typified the twins' relationship fell apart. Each brother favoured a different site. Romulus wanted to place the city on the Palatine Hill, while Remus preferred the Aventine Hill. Asking the Gods to decide the matter proved inconclusive. Each brother looked for a sign. Remus was the first to be rewarded with the sight of six auspicious birds. However, Romulus soon topped this with a sighting of 12 birds. Which flight of birds should be taken as definitive – the first one or the greater one?

The matter was never resolved because, before a ruling could be established, a fight broke out between the brothers. Remus insulted Romulus by leaping over the supposed boundary of his new city. Such provocation was too much for Romulus who lashed out at his brother, killing him. 'So perishes anybody who leaps over my walls', he declared prophetically. It is a seemingly inauspicious start to the birth of a city, but it was not unusual. As mentioned before, city-founders were a breed apart: they could be mad, bad or just dangerous to know. They were certainly never dull. In many ways, the death of Remus is a particularly appropriate motif for the start of a city in which the shedding of political blood will be a dominant feature.

Romulus not only founded a city, he also founded the institution of kingship that ruled Rome for the next six generations. The rule of these kings sees the expansion of Rome and the establishment of many of its laws, rites and civic institutions. Romulus begins this period of expansion when, to provide wives for his group of largely male followers, he abducts women from a neighbouring community (the incident is known as 'The Rape of the Sabine Women'). Like Aeneas, Romulus suffered an uncertain end. According to one version, he disappeared in a whirlwind, assuming divinity and becoming a God. Another version suggests that this story was a convenient fiction to cover up his political assassination. Romulus is a divisive figure in our sources. Fortunately for Rome, his successor Numa Pompilius proved a very different sort of king. Famed in antiquity for his wisdom and piety, the reign of Numa is regarded with affection by our sources. The vast majority of the infrastructure of Roman religion is attributed to his reign.

Numa would be the last unambiguously 'good' king of Rome. His successors, while often successful in battle, do not enjoy his virtuous reputation. Rome grew great under their rule, but their morality was often questionable. The final king of Rome, Lucius

Tarquinius Superbus ('Tarquin the Proud') exemplifies this state of decline. After usurping the throne, his reign was characterized by acts of brutality and duplicity, grandiose building projects, and overweening ambition. In this, he very much resembled the model of a typical Greek tyrant. Finally, when his son raped Lucretia, the virtuous wife of one of his commanders, and she killed herself, the people of Rome had had enough. They rose up and expelled the king.

The story of the expulsion of Tarquin marks the end of the regal period of Roman rule. It also establishes in the Roman mindset a particular abhorrence for the notion of kingship. Rome knew instinctively that she did not want kings. Working out what she wanted instead was a trickier business, and one that would trouble the Romans for the rest of their history.

▶ The Roman Republic

The history of the Roman Republic (from the Latin *res publica* – 'a thing held in common', 'a public affair') is largely a conversation about power. Who should have it? How much should they have? How should those exercising it be selected? Where should power be located? What limits should be imposed? Indeed, none of the answers that Rome offered to these questions ever seemed permanently to satisfy her. Rome remained ambivalent about the exercise of power. Every solution was revisited – sometimes almost immediately, sometimes centuries later.

Indeed, one way of telling the story of the Roman Republic is as a system continually under threat. The Republic never seems to have been without enemies and there is a dense body of rhetoric about the need for constant vigilance in defending its interests. Very quickly a Republican exemplary tradition built up to buttress the heroic stories of Gods and heroes. The courageous Horatius Cocles, who stood alone defending the bridge across the Tiber from invading forces bent on restoring a king to Rome, was joined in civic legend by Lucius Junius Brutus, who sentenced his own sons to death for attempting to overthrow the constitution, and Gaius Mucius Scaevola, who stoically thrust his hand into a roaring fire and stood there unflinching to show the enemies of Rome the type of men that they would face.

At the heart of the system of government that replaced the kingship was the consulship. This was the highest elected political office in the state. Each year two consuls were elected for one year. By dividing the office between two officers, a limit was put on their powers. Each consul had the power to veto his colleague. Such checks and balances were necessary given the tremendous powers that the consuls exercised. The consuls commanded the armies of Rome. Outside the city of Rome, their power was absolute. Citizens in the army could be exiled, fined and even put to death if the consul commanded. Within the city, their powers were much more circumscribed. Rome was now a city of citizens and all enjoyed certain inalienable rights, including the right of appeal against the decision of a magistrate. Nevertheless, the consuls were given great authority to defend and implement the laws of the state. They also exercised important diplomatic functions, introducing embassies to Rome and assisting in the negotiating of treaties.

By having the office elected and limited to just one year, the office of consul was made responsive to the will of the people. The historian Polybius (c. 200–c. 118 BC) famously described Rome as having 'a mixed constitution': one that combined monarchic, oligarchic and democratic elements. The consuls embodied the monarchic element. Their election exhibited Rome's democratic tendency.

Of course, not everyone at Rome might have agreed that the election of the consuls was particularly democratic. Rome had a complicated system of assemblies, committees and councils where her citizens met to deliberate, pass laws and elect officials. Some were more democratic than others. Some favoured the wealthy and rhetorically-educated. For example, the Assembly that voted for the consul, while open to all male citizens of military age, was heavily gerrymandered in such a way that the votes of the wealthy citizens counted for more than those of the poor. Similarly, the Roman Senate, the city's oldest and most august deliberative body, was initially only open to the elite. Even when the admission rules were relaxed and it was possible to become a senator after holding certain prescribed civic magistracies, it was still a body dominated by the old aristocratic families. The Senate always required new men to renew it, but it did not make the admission process easy. In the period of the Roman Empire, a property qualification of 1 million sesterces was required for membership of the Senate. This was an exclusive body to which only the wealthiest, best connected and morally upright could gain admission.

Balancing the concerns of the rich and the poor was an ongoing project throughout most of the period of the Roman Republic. Roman writers present a 'Struggle of the Orders' that pitched the wealthy aristocrats (the 'patricians') against the non-aristocratic, less financially-advantaged citizens (the 'plebeians'). Such claims about an ongoing struggle for over 200 years need to be treated sceptically. What these stories indicate is a trend in the development of the Roman constitution that privilege and power should be equitably distributed.

While the political organization of Rome might have radically changed from the time of the Kings, her expansionist tendencies had not. Roman domination of her immediate surroundings continued. By the beginning of the third century BC, Rome was established as the major power on the Italian peninsula.

Inevitably, expansion invited opposition. Sometimes, the opposition could be easily overcome. At other times, it proved deadly. The wars with Carthage – the Punic Wars – well demonstrate just how dangerous the opposition to Rome could be.

From North Africa the Carthaginian sphere of influence extended to Sicily, Spain, Portugal, Sardinia and Corsica. It was inevitable that Rome and Carthage should come into conflict. It was not the dead hand of Dido that brought it about so much as competing economic and political interests.

In Carthage, Rome found a foe to equal her. In a series of conflicts (264 BC to 146 BC), Rome eventually got the better of the Carthaginians, but it was a close call. Rome's generals seemed hamstrung by principles of collegiality. There was a reluctance to invest in one man. The Roman army would develop into a powerful fighting force, but in this period this band of citizen soldiers was still far from professional. Most famously, the Carthaginian commander Hannibal was able to cross the Alps with 37 elephants and ravage the Roman countryside before being beaten back by Roman forces. In practice, Hannibal's elephants gave him little tactical advantage in the campaign – many of them died crossing the Alps. However, as a symbol of Carthaginian power and tactical ingenuity, they are unbeatable. Finally, Rome defeated the North African superpower, completely wiping it out in 146 BC. The story of the 'salting' of the city is apocryphal, but it captures the totality of the destruction.

The defeat of Carthage led to an exponential increase in the area over which Rome exercised some form of control. It also drew Rome east towards the Hellenistic Kingdoms of Greece, Egypt and Asia Minor. Some of these had supported Carthage against Rome. Others sought alliances with the new emergent power in the West. Enticed by a combination of invitation and insult, Rome found herself increasingly forced (or so she liked to claim) to extend her sphere of influence. In much the same way as she had established control of Italy, through a combination of diplomacy and military aggression, she soon found herself exercising dominion over the whole Mediterranean.

The success of the Roman Republic also contained the seeds of its downfall. Roman moralists liked to point to the corrupting effect of the riches that flowed into Rome as a result of the conflicts. In a sense, they are right (and also very wrong).

The wealth that flowed into Rome led to a physical transformation in the city. More importantly, it allowed her elites to compete with each other in ways that previously would have been unimaginable. They could deploy resources that were simply unavailable to previous generations. They could bribe citizens (the so-called offer of 'Bread and Circuses') to achieve electoral outcomes for themselves and their associates. It is no accident that it is a late Roman Republican politician, Marcus Licinius Crassus, whose name is still a byword for extreme wealth. Not only did Roman elites enjoy increased personal wealth, they could reap astronomical sums through the corrupt administration of the provinces. More importantly, through a combination of political control and their own wealth, they could materially support troops and maintain their loyalty.

Changes in the organization and treatment of the army was the other factor that accelerated the end of the Republic. Rome's military expansion had seen the transformation of her army from a non-professional force of citizen soldiers into a well-organized killing machine. Furthermore, the extended duration of Rome's overseas campaigns made the troops increasingly dependent on the skills of their military leaders to provide them with a livelihood. It was the generals who controlled how the spoils of the campaign were distributed and it was generals who negotiated the financial terms which determined the rewards that veterans enjoyed on return from campaign. It is no wonder that, increasingly, the army came to be dominated by the cult of personality – where loyalty to the leader often surpassed loyalty to the State.

The politics of the Late Republic is dominated by personalities. Names such as Pompey, Sulla, Mark Antony and Julius Caesar have become justly famous (sometimes infamous), but it is always worthwhile remembering that it was the underlying social, political, economic and military structures that gave these 'great men' their stage, that motivated and funded their activities, and allowed them to prosecute their aims. Without the resources to fund their campaigns, the military skills of their soldiers or their ambitions fuelled by a culture of elite competition, they would have passed into history unnoticed.

From the last few decades of the second century BC, the Roman Republic increasingly became a competition in which the winner was the last man left standing. Political violence escalated, climaxing with the murder of Julius Caesar on the floor of the Senate. The Republican system buckled under the strain. Some politicians such as the great Roman orator Marcus Tullius Cicero (106–43 BC), genuinely seem to have thought that a revivified Republican constitution backed by the rule of law and overseen by statesmen committed to public virtue could save the Republic. Cicero's dream died when he was murdered on the orders of Mark Antony, and his head and hands placed on the speaker's platform in the Roman Forum.

Eventually only two men effectively remained: Octavian, the heir to Julius Caesar; and Julius Caesar's former ally and confidante, Mark Antony. Octavian enjoyed the support of Rome and the western part of the Roman world. Antony's support came from the East, especially Egypt and her extremely capable Queen Cleopatra VII. The fate of Rome was determined by the Battle of Actium in 31 BC when Octavian's forces defeated Antony's fleet. From that time, Octavian enjoyed dominion without opposition. More importantly, at that moment, it became possible for Octavian to implement an alternative system

▲ Portrait head of Augustus (Octavian). First century AD. (© The Trustees of the British Museum)

of rule that attempted to cure some of the structural problems of the Roman Republic. Octavian offered a new system for the arrangement of power. In place of a Republic, Rome would be transformed into an Empire.

▶ The Roman Empire

When Octavian defeated Antony, he inherited a world that was sick of political conflict and bloodshed. It was a world ripe for a new settlement and ready for a new type of politics.

Constitutional and legal historians have spilt much ink on the technical basis on which Octavian reformed the Roman State. It is easy to get lost in the minutiae of constitutional reforms and ask, by what power did Octavian effect this change, or what legislation was required to bring about this enactment? Such writing often loses sight of the reality of the political situation that Octavian enjoyed. All opposition had been crushed. Through his management of military pay, bonuses on discharge and introduction of oaths of loyalty, Octavian effectively controlled all military power. There was no popular appetite for resistance – quite the reverse in fact. Many were eager to be co-opted. In such a situation, Octavian effectively enjoyed carte blanche to reform the State.

The reason why it is easy to lose sight of the pragmatics of the situation is that Octavian went out of his way to hide it. Part of his political genius was the fact that he chose not to create a new magistracy to reflect his supreme position. All the traditional offices remained. The Senate was left intact. Rome had firmly rejected 'kings', and even magistracies that approximated kingship, such as the temporary but all-powerful emergency office of 'dictator', were viewed with suspicion. Under Octavian, power would not come from a singular office, but from an agglomeration of pre-existing offices. Over the course of his rule, we see him taking a variety of offices, often simultaneously. These magistracies provided a fig-leaf for Octavian's power – a fiction in which the Senate and People of Rome could collude in pretending that Rome was still notionally a Republic and that Octavian was not a tyrant, just 'first among equals'.

Underpinning Octavian's regime was his control of the army and the provinces. Octavian's use of the title 'imperator', from which we get the word 'emperor', reflects this. During the Early Republic, the title 'imperator' was given to a victorious commander by his troops on the battlefield. Later it came to indicate a pre-eminent military commander, and it is this sense that Octavian preserved. Almost all the significant provinces in which the army was based were controlled by him through governors ('legates') that he appointed personally. The province of Egypt was regarded as especially important in this new arrangement. The wealth of Egypt and the vital contribution that it made to Rome's grain supply meant that the new regime had to be especially careful about who controlled the province. Rather than allow it to be administered by a potentially ambitious senator, Octavian entrusted Egypt initially to a very close friend. Later, it would become practice to allocate it to a more junior official; one who could not possibly entertain ambitions to become rival to the emperor. Senators were banned from even visiting the province without permission. Only a handful of provinces remained under the notional control of the Senate – the most important being Africa and Asia (western Turkey).

Checking, or at least side-tracking, elite ambitions was the secret to maintaining Octavian's new order. In making himself the immovable centre of Roman power, Octavian both defined the limits of ambition and reoriented them. The game was now less about achieving office than about achieving proximity to Octavian. The principal offices of State were still filled, but their incumbents held them by virtue of imperial favour. Magistracies reflected political power rather than acting as springboards to it. Certain types of elite competition were removed. No longer could generals compete to be awarded a military triumph. These spectacles and tributes to martial prowess now effectively became the preserve of the emperor and his immediate family.

The complicity of the Senate in this new vision is reflected in the titles that they heaped upon Octavian. In 27 BC, he was given the titles of Augustus ('illustrious one', the name by which Octavian is now best known) and Princeps ('first citizen'). To these was later added Pater Patriae ('Father of the Country').

The recipe for rule developed by Octavian proved to be a popular and influential one. Cemented into place by his long period of leadership (over 40 years), this system of government came to be seen as the only viable form of administration. Some writers might look back with wistful nostalgia on the period of the Republic and evoke its memory as a form of opposition to the overtly dictatorial rule of their own day, but nobody actively or genuinely worked for its restoration.

As power was now defined by proximity to the emperor, the family of the emperor grew in importance. One of the by-products of imperial systems of government is the way in which it creates a space for women to exercise power and influence. The wives and daughters of the emperor grew in prominence, prestige and authority. Livia, the wife of Octavian, was granted a public statue, and following Octavian's death she was awarded numerous honours by cities that wanted to honour her and her husband.

The cult of personality that grew up around the figure of the emperor had a number of effects. At one extreme, it became a literal cult, especially in the East where, since the time of Alexander, there had been a tradition of ruler-cult. A number of emperors were worshipped as Gods either during their lifetimes or after their deaths. It also meant that there was greater focus on the personality of the emperor. Through coins, monuments, statues and building projects, emperors began consciously to shape their public personae. The emperor became a source of spectacle. He also became the subject of gossip. In a regime where intimacy equates with power, there is clearly much to be gained by claiming to have discrete knowledge of the private lives of imperial personages. It is this feature that helps explain the gossipy nature of so much of ancient writing about emperors. Romans loved scandal, not exclusively out of a desire for titillation, but because such scandal allowed them access to the centre of power.

Bad emperors always prove more memorable than good ones. The tales of the debauchery on Capri of Octavian's successor Tiberius became legend. Nero playing the lyre while Rome burnt, Caligula planning to make his horse a consul, Messalina, wife of the Emperor Claudius, challenging the whores of Rome in a sex contest – all belong to the rich imperial biographical tradition that arose from Rome's centralized political system.

If one were to confine one's reading only to imperial biography, it would seem a miracle that the Roman Empire proved as successful as it did. All the emperors (even the good ones) seem megalomaniacal narcissists. One has to search very hard for imperial wives and daughters who are not cruel, crazed or over-sexed. Only in the flattery of imperial panegyric do we find unequivocally positive portraits of imperial figures. In this respect, biography represents a dangerous distortion. We know, for example, that emperors such as Nero who suffered at the merciless hand of biographers were actually much loved and admired by large sections of the population. Nero's popularity in Greece, for example, was unparalleled. Even decades after death, 'false Neros' were sighted popping up in the East as part of a general hope for the emperor's return.

In some ways the irrelevance of the personality of the emperor to the system of government is demonstrated by the fact that the Empire remained so stable despite the number of dynastic changes that it endured. The dynasty established by Octavian, the so-called Julio-Claudian dynasty (27 BC–AD 68), gave way to the Flavians (AD 69–96), who were in turn succeeded by the Antonines (AD 96–192) and then the Severans (AD 193–235). Yet while the shift from one dynasty was inevitably rough and chaotic – in AD 69 there were four substantial rivals for the emperorship and in AD 193 there were five claimants – these moments of disruption were comparatively short and each was followed by a period of relative peace in which the imperial system reasserted itself. It is only in the third century AD that we see a sustained period of conflict and civil war. However, even here, the scholarly trend is to see this period as less bleak than was once imagined. Yet, it is striking that the emperor who emerged from this chaos, Diocletian (AD c. 245–c. 311), did not undertake a wholesale abandonment of the Augustan imperial system. Instead, he modified it, introducing a system of junior co-emperors so that the Empire was administered by four ('The Tetrarchy'). More emperors, not fewer.

What the biographical tradition ignores is the tremendous structural benefits that Rome brought to her provinces and cities during the imperial period. Moreover, these benefits were benefits that Rome was not reluctant to share. Unlike Athens, for example, who jealously guarded her gift of citizenship, Rome was not exclusive in relation to whom she awarded citizenship or civic rights. The process of extending civic rights to non-Romans began in the Republic when first the surrounding Italian communities were incorporated into the State. Gradually these rights were extended to more and more regions. The process of extension of Roman citizenship reached its climax in the Edict of Caracalla, the law passed by the Roman Emperor Caracalla in AD 212, which said that all free people in the Roman Empire should be given citizenship.

Promoting trade, improving systems of transport, removing the scourge of piracy, acting as an intermediary so that regional conflicts did not descend into bloody conflict – there was much for the provincial to enjoy about Roman rule. For the lower orders, the Roman army provided a route for social mobility. Moreover, the Romans tended to work within local systems of government rather than imposing a centralized model. Local customs and laws were accommodated as much as possible. Rome worked with local elites, often making the most prominent members of the community full Roman citizens. The benefits they bestowed upon them were significant and these local elites often became Rome's most enthusiastic supporters.

Of course, it is practically impossible to exercise power without encountering resistance. Sometimes this resistance could be passive and small scale. The Greeks, for example, could be very snide about their Roman masters, mocking them for their seemingly uncouth ways. At other times, resistance could take a far more dramatic turn. The revolts of the British Queen Boudica (c. AD 15–61) following the annexation of her kingdom by a Roman official resulted in the wholesale destruction of the Roman town of Camulodunum (Colchester) and the razing of the temple dedicated to the Emperor Claudius. Verulamium (St Albans) would also fall to Boudica's troops before she was finally defeated in battle.

As Boudica's troops discovered, Rome was not averse to crushing dissent when needed. Yet, even here Roman punishments tend to be spectacular and exemplary rather than genocidal. Only those who were seen as irreconcilably opposed to incorporation within the Roman state were punished severely. So, for example, the Jews who refused to acknowledge the supremacy of the emperor and revolted against Roman rule would see their temple destroyed, their cities flattened, and ultimately their dispersal from the city of Jerusalem. The historian Cassius Dio claimed that over 580,000 Jews were killed in the final attack against Judea. The number is most likely an exaggeration. Yet, it helps to give scale to the power of Roman anger should it arise. The Roman historian Tacitus has a provincial opposed to Roman rule decry that the Romans 'make a wasteland and call it peace'. To those implacably opposed to the Empire, the words were ominously true.

4

Women and slaves

'Of all creatures that draw breath, women are the most wretched ... Men say that we live a carefree life at home while they fight with the spear. How wrong they are! I would rather stand three times with a shield in battle than give birth once.'

Euripides, *Medea* (230–50)

'We are all Greeks', declared the poet Percy Bysshe Shelley. The declaration came in the 1822 Preface to his verse drama 'Hellas', in which Shelley attempted to elicit support for the cause of Greek freedom in the fight against Ottoman control. In the course of the drama, loosely inspired by Aeschylus' tragedy *The Persians*, a chorus of enslaved Greek women laments their fate at the Ottoman court. We are supposed to sympathize with their wretched plight. Yet, there is a certain irony here. Arguably, the life of Ottoman slaves and women was no worse than the lives of many slaves and women in ancient Greece. It is easy for a well-off free man to imagine himself as an ancient Greek, but would Shelley wish the same fate on his second wife, Mary? It is hard to imagine the daughter of Mary Wollstonecraft, the leading advocate of women's rights, being content with the restricted life of an Athenian wife. Certainly, the life of a Greek woman would have offered little opportunity for the author of *Frankenstein* to produce her voluminous literary output.

Looking at the lives of women and slaves in antiquity is one of the moments where we feel the distance between us and the Greeks and Romans. The implicit assumptions that supported the institution of slavery and female exclusion from public life are appalling. Yet they run to the core of the culture. Greece and Rome, together historically with the Caribbean, the American Old South and Brazil, belong to a group of cultures that modern historians call 'slave cultures'. By this they mean not just that the cultures had slaves, but that the ownership and trade of slaves was so integral to the economic, legal and social fabric of the society that without slaves the culture would not function. Without slaves, Greece and Rome would be radically altered, they would become unrecognizable. We could make a similar claim about their treatment of women. Confronting the role and status of women and slaves in the ancient world can take us to some dark places. They are a reminder that behind 'the glory that was Greece' and 'the grandeur that was Rome' was an often unpleasant reality.

▶ The silent women of Athens

The quotation at the start of Chapter 2 is from the funeral oration for the war dead, delivered by the Athenian statesman Pericles; this speech is held up as a model of democratic rhetoric. Over the course of the speech, Pericles praises Athens for her culture, liberalism and inclusiveness. However, there are limits to his invitation to share in the bounty of Athens. For, at the end of this speech, there is a sting in the tail for the grieving widows. After consoling the fathers, brothers and sons, Pericles turns to the women and says, 'If I must say anything on female virtue to those who are now widowed, let it be these few words. Your glory will be great if you do not prove to be worse than your innate nature, and the greatest glory will come to the woman who is least talked about by men whether for good or bad.' Put simply, the best women are the silent ones, those who go unnoticed.

For citizens of modern democracies, Pericles' words come as a shock, especially given the warmth of the rhetoric that precedes them. Yet, they are a stark reminder that Athens was very much an exclusive male club. Athenians were not shy in hiding their misogyny. A fourth-century BC orator boasted that Athenian men 'have prostitutes for sex, mistresses for conversation, and wives for the production of children.' He expected his large (all male) jury to nod their heads in agreement. Women in Athens could not vote and their ability to own property was limited. The law refused to enforce agreements made with a woman where the value of the contract was greater than the equivalent of a couple of sacks of wheat.

From the moment of their birth, women were under the permanent control of a male guardian. Initially, this was their father and in his absence either a brother or uncle. Later, it would be her husband. The production of children was considered the primary goal of a woman's life. Men feared dying without an heir. The man who left a 'barren' household was considered a failure. For this reason, marriage occurred early for girls, normally beginning around the age of 14, as soon as it was possible for them to conceive. Husbands were usually much older, around the age of 30. Such a difference in age inevitably translated into a difference in power. Even the most indulgent Athenian husbands cannot help sounding extremely condescending when speaking about their wives.

Buttressing this disempowerment of women was a panoply of stories, anecdotes, stereotypes and scientific observations. According to myth, the 'first woman' Pandora was created by the Gods as punishment for Prometheus stealing fire from the Gods and giving it to man. 'An evil for mortal men' is how the poet Hesiod puts it. It is no coincidence that Athena, the principal goddess of Athens, was not born of a woman. Instead, she emerged from Zeus' head, armoured and fully-formed. She shares none of the weaknesses typically ascribed to women.

It was their weak will that justified women's disenfranchisement. Women were constructed as creatures of appetite. They lacked the self-control of men. It was for this reason that women needed to be under constant guardianship. Women's appetites for food, drink and sex were legendary. They were infamous for enjoying sex more than men. The seer Tiresias who, owing to a magical metamorphosis, spent time as both a man and a woman, was turned blind by Hera for letting this secret out. In a quote attributed to the medical writer Galen, he declares that 'every animal is sad after coitus except the human female and the rooster.' It was this unbridled sexual appetite that justified the constant supervision of women. Women could not be trusted. Citizen women rarely left the house. When they did so, they were often veiled.

Female bodies were viewed as potentially dangerous or disordered. In the medical writers we find the idea of the 'wandering womb', in which the womb is considered almost like an independent animal that could move about the body. It could respond to smells, being attracted by sweet smells and repulsed by fetid ones. As it wandered, it caused all sorts of problems from headaches to nose bleeds to knee problems. This idea of the female body as potentially monstrous perhaps explains why so many of our most famous Greek monsters (e.g. Medusa, Scylla, Charybdis, Harpies, Sirens) are female.

Of course, the Greeks knew on one level that all these constructions were convenient social fictions. It is noticeable that writers are always most misogynist about other peoples' wives and daughters. Their own women are always models of virtue. The epitaphs on tombstones show touching devotion to mothers and wives. On the stage, the Athenians were prepared to grant women more latitude. Here we find the great tragic heroines such as Antigone, Electra or Medea: women who are prepared to stand up to men, often with justice on their side. The important religious roles given to women who served as priestess of various cults related to the Greek goddesses, as well as their role in state festivals such as the festivals for Dionysus and Athena, also show a different side to the bleak picture painted by legal texts and economic documents.

Athens was particularly invested in a high level of misogyny because ideologically she needed to justify excluding women from democracy. Other non-democratic states did not have this problem, and there we see women enjoying far more rights and freedoms. Sparta offers an obvious comparison with

Athens. Here women enjoyed many more rights and freedoms. They could own property. They were far more outspoken than their Athenian counterparts. Girls would observe the boys in their training and ridicule those underperforming. The biographer Plutarch collected the sayings of Spartan women into an essay. It is telling that there is no extant Athenian equivalent. In this collection, we find the famous injunction that mothers gave to their sons when they handed them their shield: 'Come back either with it [in victory] or on it [in death].' Plutarch's essay also includes the famous exchange between an Athenian woman and a Spartan: 'Why is it that you Spartan women are the only women that lord it over your men?' 'Because we are the only women who give birth to men,' came the reply.

All this changed with the beginning of the Hellenistic period. The transition from city-states to kingdoms had a profound impact on the status of women. Royal women, through their influence with their husbands and fathers, grew in status and the effect trickled down so that the wives of governors and generals also gained in importance. In this period, we have a number of accounts of women amassing large fortunes in their own right. One even used her wealth to establish a cult so that her descendants, if they wished to share in their inheritance, needed to offer her spirit sacrifices as if she were a hero. It is from this world of high status, savvy, politically-engaged, economically-literate women that rulers such as the indomitable Cleopatra VII, the woman who captivated both Julius Caesar and Mark Antony, will emerge.

▶ The slaves of Greece

At some point in the early part of the fourth century BC, a disabled citizen was denied the dole to which he was entitled. We have the speech written for him protesting the decision to remove him from the list of state pensioners. It is a remarkable document. We possess so few documents that seem to belong to the genuinely poor. As proof of his poverty, the citizen offers a compelling piece of evidence. He is so poor that he cannot even afford a slave. It is a telling admission. Slave ownership was so ubiquitous that only the poorest, most destitute of citizens could not afford at least one slave.

Our earliest references to Greek slaves occur in the Mycenaean Linear B tablets, and slaves can be found in the Homeric texts. Primarily, the slaves of the *Odyssey* and the *Iliad* are women – prizes captured as booty during conflict. However, we do have some male slaves as well. The most famous one is the kind and generous swineherd Eumaeus, who is the first person to welcome Odysseus (although he does not recognize him) to Ithaca. Eumaeus ended up a slave not through capture in war, but through deliberate enslavement by a passing trader who seduced his nurse.

Warfare and commercial slaving provided the majority of Greek slaves. People needed to be careful as they moved about the Mediterranean. Your rights as a free person were never guaranteed. The moment you set one foot beyond your city's boundaries you risked losing all your freedom and property. In one infamous case, we are told of a master who pursued his runaway slaves to a nearby town only to find himself enslaved by the inhabitants. In the end, his family was forced to buy him from his enslavers to restore his freedom. It was for this reason that the Greeks made the provision of hospitality and respect to strangers such an important social virtue. Without it, nobody could risk travel.

The life of a slave varied tremendously according to the tasks they were assigned and the nature of their master. On the whole, our evidence suggests that they were not overly mistreated. In a largely subsistence economy, a slave represented a significant investment. There was a strong economic incentive to ensure that your slave was reasonably content and in good condition. Masters and slaves often worked alongside each other. Some slaves enjoyed a tremendous degree of autonomy. Slaves could act as foreign agents for merchants, effectively running large-scale enterprises in distant ports. Public slaves (i.e. slaves who were owned by the city rather than individual masters) lived independent lives. They rented their own apartments. They were required to report to the magistrate they served for work each morning, but otherwise their time was their own. One notorious public slave in the fourth century was infamous for spending his leisure hours gambling, drinking and betting on cockfights. He even took a citizen boy lover.

Skilled slaves, particularly those with a talent for business, could end up being rewarded with their freedom. There is one famous case of a slave in the fourth century who, through commercial transactions, made his owner so much money that he was rewarded with his freedom. As a free man, he continued to increase his fortune, so much so that, after a series of generous endowments to the city, he was awarded citizenship. In the next generation, his son went on to become one of Athens' leading politicians. Sometimes slaves just needed to be at the right place at the right time. Athens could be generous towards her slaves. The slaves that fought for Athens at the battle of Arginusae during the Peloponnesian War were rewarded with their freedom and possibly even citizenship.

Of course, such cases represent the exception. As Eumaeus observes in the *Odyssey*, 'Zeus takes away half a man's virtue, when he becomes a slave.' Inevitably, free citizens felt superior to slaves and they justified this superiority on moral and biological grounds. The most extreme example of the latter position was Aristotle who declared that there are some people who, by their nature, are born to be slaves. It was a free man's duty to enslave such people. It is unclear how many people shared Aristotle's idea of natural slavery. Clearly, there was prejudice against slaves. Like women, slaves needed to be watched. They could not be trusted. The scheming slave was a staple of Attic comedy. In Athenian law, evidence from slaves was only admissible if it had been obtained by torture. You could not trust a slave to just speak the truth.

▶ Roman matrons

On the surface, the legal position of women in Rome seems not dissimilar to the situation that obtained in Athens. Once again, we see a large role played by legal guardians. Cicero jokes that, 'it was due to their mental infirmity that our ancestors determined that all women should be under the control of their guardians'. This may tempt us to see Roman women as living like their Athenian counterparts in a perpetually infantilized state without rights. The reality was far more complex. For example, it is worth remembering that it was not just daughters who were under the complete control of their fathers. The same regime applied to sons as well. In theory, fathers had the power of life and death over all their children, no matter what their age. Sons may have had the right to enter into financial contracts, but technically all the goods that they acquired were the property of their father. The legal disabilities suffered by women look not too dissimilar to those that operated for large numbers of men. The power that Rome gave to its fathers was extraordinary and, while few fathers seem to have exercised the full range of punitive powers available to them, Rome went to great lengths to protect these rights. The son or daughter who defied their father was a reviled figure. Even worse was the child who took the father's life. Rome could imagine no worse crime. The penalty for such an act was being sewn into a sack and thrown in a river to drown. Some versions of the punishment have the perpetrator beaten with rods and his mouth gagged before he is thrown into the sack with an assortment of animals such as a dog, a cock, a viper and a monkey. It was a ghastly way to die. The Emperor Augustus did his best to avoid ever having to impose the penalty even in cases of obvious guilt.

Moreover, the status of women was a constantly evolving issue over the course of Roman history. Take, for example, an issue like marriage. Together with motherhood, marriage represented the primary aim of a woman's life. The respectful and respectable Roman matron was often held up as a female paradigm. Rome recognized two forms of marriage. The first, and earlier, was marriage 'in the hand', in which the father or guardian transferred his power into 'the hands' of the husband. As a result, the husband now had all the powers over his wife that her father enjoyed. The wife became legally separated from her birth family and was effectively adopted into her husband's family. In such circumstances, divorce, though possible, was difficult, and the dowry that she brought with her was harder to retrieve. However, this form of marriage gradually came to be replaced by a second form of marriage in which none of the father's powers were transferred. The bride did not come under the legal control of her husband, divorce was easier to obtain, and the process for the return of a dowry was more straightforward. Over time, we see a similar loosening of restrictions on women's right to make wills, deal with property and divorce.

Of course, the legal framework was only one factor that governed women's lives. Economic conditions, cultural practices, social status, religious obligations and political circumstances all impacted on the role fulfilled by women in Rome. As a result, some women feature more prominently than others. The Vestal Virgins, for example, regularly appear in our sources, firstly because their unusual nature made them a source of fascination even in antiquity and, secondly, because of their importance to the city of Rome. This group of six priestesses was charged with tending the 'undying fire' in the temple of Vesta, the goddess of the hearth, in the centre of Rome. This was a crucial task. Should the fire ever go out, it was a sign of impending doom for Rome. They also enjoyed a series of unique privileges. On becoming a Vestal, normally between the age of six and ten, the girl was freed from the power of her father. She needed no guardian, although she was technically under the control of the Pontifex Maximus ('High Priest') of Rome. A Vestal could own property. Crassus, for example, hounded a Vestal who owned a luxurious villa that he desired. Vestals were granted special seats in the theatre, a litter to transport them around the city, and a bodyguard. It was a capital offence to pass beneath a Vestal's litter in the street. Such freedoms came at a price. She was forced to remain a virgin for the 30 years of her service. Breaches of chastity were punished severely, with the Vestal being entombed alive.

Other women come to prominence because they became emblematic of Roman female virtues or vices. When we discussed the transition from Roman Republic to Empire, we noted the often scandalous reputation that Roman imperial women enjoyed. Yet, the picture is not completely one of dishonourable and unprincipled women. There was equally a set repertoire of noble women invoked by orators as inspirational examples. These include Lucretia, whose rape and subsequent suicide, was the spark that led to the overthrow of the Kings of Rome; Cloelia, who refused to be held hostage by Rome's enemies and battled swirling waters and a hail of arrows to escape; the mother of Coriolanus, who braved enemy lines to bring this renegade general to heel when he threatened Rome; and Cornelia, the highly literate mother of Tiberius and Gaius Gracchus, two of Rome's leading reformers during the Roman Republic.

Getting beyond the stereotypes of the 'good' and 'bad' woman is difficult. Our texts are written by men for men and they are always constrained by the rules of genre. If we look at tombstone and grave epitaphs, we see numerous testaments to virtuous, much loved, often financially capable women. It is a wonderful picture, but, sadly, as reliable as reconstructing family relations from Mother's Day cards. Conversely, examine Roman love poetry and these chaste wives turn out to be often artful adulterers, inspiring numerous scandalous verses from their besotted lovers. Worse, when the relationship goes sour, they become sluttish nymphomaniacs. 'Give to my girl, no nice words while she embraces her three hundred adulterous lovers at one time, truly loving none, but repeatedly breaking the loins of all,' Catullus spits poetically at his former lover. The Roman genre of satire was even worse. Here the poet adopted the persona of a curmudgeonly, aggrieved spectator railing against the iniquities of the world. Along with slaves, foreigners and the wealthy, women do not come out well in this genre. In his famous satire on women, Juvenal paints a terrible portrait of Rome's women. They escape at night to urinate on the shrine of the goddess of chastity, they run away with deformed gladiators, they avoid breastfeeding lest it deform their breasts, and conspire to arrange abortions to disguise their affairs. Again, the mistake would be to think that any of this verse even approximates reality.

▶ Slavery in Rome

Like women, generalizing about slaves in Rome is difficult. At their peak, slaves represented one third of the population of Italy. Within a single wealthy household, there might be many hundreds of slaves. According to the satirist Juvenal, practically the first question you ask when determining somebody's wealth is, 'how many slaves do they own?' The slaves of Rome came from places as diverse as India, Nubia, Greece, Syria, Germany, Britain and Egypt. Some were extremely well-educated, others were illiterate. Their jobs could involve crippling manual labour or they could enjoy comfortable, well-appointed managerial positions. The lives of slaves were as wide-ranging as the roles they fulfilled.

The only fact that unites slaves is their legal status. However, much freedom they enjoyed, they still remained the property of their master. Their legal rights were few. They could be punished, even killed, without sanction. They could be traded at will. They were forbidden to marry, although they could cohabit. Children born of slaves became the property of their master. Only in death did slaves find some measure of equality. Slaves enjoyed the right of burial and it was a responsibility of the master to ensure that a slave received a proper burial. We possess numerous inscriptions from tombs of slaves and these are invaluable documents that allow us to flesh out the lives of figures that our historical accounts all too often ignore.

Clearly, life for slaves could be terrible. We do not have to look hard to find acts of extraordinary cruelty. Some masters, such as Vedius Pollio, became infamous for their cruelty. Supposedly, he kept a pool of lampreys to which he fed slaves that displeased him. Yet, in some ways, it is the regular, unremarkable brutality that is so alarming. Many of our sources treat the beating of slaves as an unexceptional occurrence. We have accounts of slaves being hung up by their hands with weights attached to their feet, or placed in stocks. The civilized Emperor Hadrian even stabbed out a slave's eye with a stylus in anger. The Roman statesman Cato was famous both for his Republican virtues and his mistreatment of slaves; working them hard like animals and then selling them off the moment they fell sick or grew old. Mistresses could be equally as cruel to their female slaves as masters to their male slaves. Given such a situation, it seems reasonable that a number of slaves would want to escape. Owners regularly complain about runaway slaves. There were even professional slave-catchers who specialized in hunting down fugitive slaves for reward.

▲ Slave collar. The inscription reads: 'I have run away; hold me. When you shall have returned me to my master, Zoninus, you will receive a gold coin.' (Museo Nazionale Romano nelle Terme di Diocleziano, Rome)

Occasionally, life for slaves could become so intolerable that they were forced to lash out. Sometimes this took the form of passive resistance, such as working inefficiently or sabotaging equipment. Even more rarely, this resistance took a more violent course and slaves openly attacked their masters. When this occurred, the consequences could be catastrophic. In AD 61, the prefect of Rome was stabbed to death by one of his slaves. The motives remain unclear. According to one account, the master reneged on a promise of freedom. In another account, the slave was jealous of the master over a love affair. Under Roman law, not only was the slave guilty of the crime, but the death penalty applied to all slaves in the household on the basis that they either knew about the plot against their master's life and did nothing, or they should have been there to protect him when he was killed. The prefect's household contained 400 slaves and there were naturally some qualms about enforcing such a massacre. It is perhaps a reflection of Roman paranoia about their slaves that, after debate, the Senate decided to carry out the death penalty. It must be said that the decision was not universally popular and Nero did need to call in troops to quell popular disturbances and to enforce the decision.

While individual acts of resistance by maltreated slaves would seem not infrequent, we see only a few instances of wholesale rebellion. A number of factors prevented slaves from joining together to oppose their masters. The ethnic and cultural diversity of slaves made unity difficult. They were also often divided among a large number of households, which made planning hard. It was only in the agricultural areas of Sicily and central Italy, where there were large numbers of culturally homogenous slaves on expansive estates, that we find conditions ripe for rebellion. During the period of the Roman Republic, we see three large-scale slave rebellions (the so-called 'Servile Wars). The last of these was the rebellion organized by Spartacus which terrorized Rome and Italy in 73–71 BC.

Little is known about Spartacus himself. Legends about him quickly sprang up, especially as Rome began to adjust to the idea of a lowly slave causing such trouble.

Traditionally, he is described as a Thracian gladiator. He may also have been a former Roman auxiliary soldier. According to one of the myths, when he first arrived in Rome a snake curled about his head while he slept – a sign, which his prophetess wife interpreted, of his impending greatness.

Initially, Spartacus' rebellion was limited to a group of gladiators from Capua who fled their gladiatorial school and sought refuge on Mount Vesuvius. However, he was soon joined by numerous agricultural slaves so that, at its height, his army numbered between 70,000 and 120,000. In 73 BC he defeated two Roman commanders, and the following year the two consuls and their armies that had been sent out to deal with the rebellion. Spartacus and his army ravaged the Italian countryside, ranging from the north to the south. Eventually, he was betrayed by some pirates with whom he negotiated transport, and Spartacus found himself trapped in the toe of Italy. Here the commander Marcus Licinius Crassus was finally able to draw Spartacus into a pitched battle and defeat him. Although Spartacus died in this encounter his body was never found.

Part of the reason why such rebellions were uncommon was that, while slaves had few rights and could, as we have seen, be subject to terrible punishments, masters on the whole treated them comparatively well. The stories about cruelty to slaves are countered by stories of generosity and kindness. We have a number of accounts of slaves who were so loyal to their masters that they refused to condemn them even under torture. Such loyalty earned rewards. Romans, for example, were far more likely to free their slaves than either Classical or Hellenistic Greeks. Indeed, the freedmen and freedwomen of Rome constitute an important social class. Their lives were regulated by the law. They were bound to their former masters by a number of important obligations. They were forbidden from taking legal action against their master nor could they give evidence against him. Should their master find himself in need, they were obliged to help him practically or financially. The freedman who possessed over 100,000 sesterces was required to leave some of his estate to his former master unless the freedman had three or more children. The relationship between a master and his freedmen often remained strong. We find a number of freedmen buried in the family tombs of their former masters. Masters marrying their freedwomen is also a documented phenomenon.

The imperial government also made extensive use of imperial freedmen who managed the emperor's correspondence, responded to petitions and administered imperial property. Over time, this group of officials began to gain increasing importance as their duties and powers expanded. These freedman became notable figures in their own right and the subjects of gossipy speculation. Emperors seen to be too reliant on their freedman were perceived as weak and ineffectual. No matter how high they rose or how efficiently they served, the taint of slavery was hard to remove.

Women and slaves

Greek drama

'The art of comedy is to portray people worse than they are in real life, the aim of tragedy is to make them appear better.'

Aristotle, Greek philosopher (384–322 BC)

▶ Alas, poor Crassus

The Roman general Marcus Licinius Crassus (c. 115–53 BC) had given exceptional service to the Roman state. Spartacus' rebellion had caused havoc in Italy until Crassus and his legions defeated this army of mutinous slaves. Yet, for ambitious politicians of Crassus' generation, the lure of greater honours and further riches was impossible to ignore. In 53 BC, hungry for further glory, Crassus invaded Parthia.

It was a terrible mistake. Parthia was one of the few powers that could stand against the might of Rome. The Parthian elite ruled an ethnically diverse and cosmopolitan empire. Crassus was not attacking wild barbarians but a sophisticated and highly cultured community.

The Parthians were also skilled fighters. Their horsemanship was legendary, as was their skill at archery. Refusing a decisive engagement, the Parthians harassed the Roman troops with arrows and spears in the inhospitable land of Mesopotamia. Beaten back to the town of Carrhae, Crassus sought to negotiate a withdrawal, but was killed in a skirmish.

This was not the end to Crassus' humiliations. His body was mutilated, and his head cut off and sent to the Parthian King. By an unfortunate coincidence, the head's arrival coincided with the staging of a production of Euripides' tragedy *The Bacchae*. When Crassus' head appeared at the Parthian court, an enterprising actor seized the trophy and made it a prop in the performance. It was grisly, macabre ending for such a leading Roman.

The story of the death of Crassus and the abuse of his head is found in the biographer Plutarch's *Life of Crassus*. Is it true? It seems unlikely. What is important to note is that the story was entirely plausible to Plutarch's audience. Such was the privileged position enjoyed by Greek drama – they would have no trouble believing that the words of Euripides still resonated here, in a barbarian court, many centuries after the work had premiered on the Athenian stage. It was impossible to imagine civilization without theatre.

▶ Performing for Dionysus

According to Aristotle (or, more correctly, one of the later scholars who summarized Aristotle), Greek drama began with a man called 'Thespis', hence the modern 'thespian' as a synonym for 'actor'. In this account, drama originally consisted only of a singing chorus. The songs that they sang were stories about the God Dionysus or songs in praise of his gifts of wine and fertility. It was Thespis who in 534 BC introduced the first actor who stood apart from the chorus and interacted with it. This proved a revolutionary move: now these stories could be told in a more dramatic form. In time, playwrights would add a second and then a third actor until the full acting complement was created. Thespis also introduced the tradition of these actors each using linen masks to play different roles. There might only be three actors, but a wide variety of roles could be played. This creates something of a scholarly game: given that there can only be three speaking actors on the stage at any one time, which roles must each of the three actors have played? These calculations can produce some seemingly perverse results. In one play, for example, owing to the exigencies of having certain characters on the stage at certain moments, the actor playing a vengeful son also has to play the mother he longs to murder.

Aristotle favours Thespis as the father of Greek drama. Others were not so sure. Plato thought it wrong to attribute the origins of acting to Thespis. For him, drama was a much older tradition; one whose origins were lost. Others preferred a more divine origin for the art form, giving an active and prominent role to Dionysus and his rites in the story of the development of drama.

Certainly, religion was central to the performance of Greek drama in Athens. Plays were performed not as individual entertainments, but as part of the celebration of a religious festival in honour of Dionysus. There were a number of such festivals in Athens. The principal one was called the Great Dionysia and it was held in March. Planning for the festival began in autumn of the previous year. It was then that the magistrate responsible for the festival called for dramatists to propose plays for inclusion in the programme. Three tragedians and between three and five (the number varies over time) writers of comedy were chosen. Each tragedian was commissioned to produce three tragedies and an obscene farce called a satyr-play. These would be performed all on one day of the festival. Only one comedy was required from each comic poet and these comedies were staged after the conclusion of the tragedies and satyr-play.

To fund the production the State selected wealthy individuals to shoulder the burden of the costs. The State paid for the actors, but all other costs of staging the play (training the chorus, costumes, etc.) were paid by the benefactor. This reliance on wealthy sponsorship was a fairly typical way of covering state expenditure on public works in Athens. Athens did not have any system of income tax, so the city relied on wealthy individuals to equip warships, maintain public gymnasia, support a team of athletes at the Olympic Games, and pay for festival banquets. The wealthy did not have much choice in the matter. These financial burdens or 'liturgies' (Gk. *leitourgia*, 'work for the people') were mandated by law. There was only a limited right of appeal, whereby a wealthy citizen could nominate a replacement if he thought that the replacement was a wealthier man than himself.

To the outsider it seems surprising that the wealthy did not object more about these costs imposed by the State. Part of the reason for the lack of dissent was the extraordinary gap between rich and poor in Athens. Those wealthy individuals who were liable for liturgies were extremely wealthy. The funds that Athens demanded were considerable, but they were not demanded every year and these individuals could afford it. Additionally, the city rewarded these citizens with honours for their public benefactions. There was considerable pride attached to acquitting your liturgy well. Wealthy citizens would compete unofficially with each other as to who had equipped the finest warship. And when it came to drama, these competitions were official. Judges were selected by lot by the magistrate in charge of organizing the festival. After 468 BC, these judges were the elected generals of Athens.

The Great Dionysia festival began with the statue of the God Dionysus being taken from his temple to the borders of Attica. From there he was reintroduced into the Athenian State. On the following day, there was an elaborate procession with the statue to the theatre so that Dionysus too could watch the show. Songs were sung and giant replicas of erect phalluses accompanied the statue as it made its way through the city. A large sacrifice was then made to the God. In one account, 240 bulls were sacrificed to Dionysus. After the sacrifice, the next days were dedicated to competitions in his honour. These included choral songs as well as dramatic performances. The choral songs were just as important as the drama, possibly even more so. Each of the ten tribes of Athens provided 50 boys and 50 men to compete in these competitions. As a result, each year as much as 5 per cent of the total Athenian citizen population was involved in singing for Dionysus.

That's 5 per cent of the male population. As so often the case with Athenian public life, theatre was very much a male affair. The actors were male (even those playing female parts) and the audience was almost exclusively male. The evidence that we have for women in the audience is slim. If they were present, they were regarded as inconsequential. This imbalance creates some intriguing dynamics. In Euripides' *Medea*, for example, the male audience watches a chorus of men playing women watch men observe a woman (played by a man) kill her children. Attempting to unravel the gender implications of such moments is inevitably going to be complicated. When Medea laments the lot of women, in whose voice is she speaking?

The location for all this activity was the theatre of Dionysus, located on the south slopes of the Athenian Acropolis. Visitors to the site today see a large semi-circular stone theatre. It is an impressive sight, but it was not the theatre of classical Athens. This stone theatre was built much later, with many elements coming from the Roman period. Initially, most of the spectators would have simply sat on the hillside. Wooden benches were added later. In front of the seats there was a flattened area called the orchestra (lit. 'dancing place') where the ancient chorus would have danced and sung. Behind the orchestra was a wooden building – the skene – that acted as a storeroom and platform upon which simple scenery could be placed. Later the skene would evolve into a stage on which actors could perform and more elaborate sets be constructed. The theatre of the golden age of Attic drama was a simple affair. The texts that it staged were so powerful that they did not need elaborate props or baroque special effects to profoundly move and challenge the audience.

▶ Tragedy

For Plato, 'tragedy is the most popularly delightful and soul-enthralling branch of poetry'. He was not alone in the judgement. Few texts have the impact of Greek tragedies. The Athenians felt its power: these plays could overwhelm. The Athenian statesman Solon supposedly regarded tragedy as having such pernicious influence that he tried to ban its performance. It was possible to feel tragedy too keenly. One of the reasons that tragedy is always set in the mythic past is that the Athenians feared that the audience would find contemporary references all too traumatic. They knew this from experience. In the first decade of the fifth century BC, the poet Phrynichus had produced a tragedy showing the brutalities inflicted by the Persians on the town of Miletus at the start of the Persians Wars. The Athenian audience found it too much. They openly wept in the theatre. The poet was fined the equivalent of three and a half years' wages and no other plays were commissioned that depicted the savagery of contemporary events. Tragedy did not just tell you a story – it enacted it, made it present, made it real. Herodotus might tell you about the crimes of the Persians, but seeing them performed was a very different experience. It is because of this vital presence of tragedy that almost all tragedies are set in the distant past and, often, in foreign cities like Troy, Argos or Thebes.

Generalizing about Greek tragedy is difficult. Even Aristotle, that great specialist in definition, struggled with summarizing the essential aspects of tragedy. In the *Poetics* he offered a number of observations about tragedy, but finding points that cover all tragedies remains a challenge. For example, we could – following Aristotle – offer this summary of tragedy: tragedies involve good and noble people who through some mistake bring about a radical transformation in their fortunes so that they lose all their happiness and prosperity; and, for the audience watching this downfall, the experience is so emotionally draining that, at the end, they feel cleansed and purged. Such a definition would encapsulate a large number of tragedies, but it would not capture them all. For example, it does not sum up a work like Euripides' *Ion*, where a long lost son is reunited with his mother, or Euripides' *Iphigenia in Tauris*, where a brother discovers that his sister, presumed killed by their father, is alive and well and living in a barbarian land from which he rescues her. For different reasons Aeschylus' *Persians* also does not quite fit the definition. This play celebrates the Athenian victory over the Persians at the decisive naval battle at Salamis, and while the play certainly involves a story of downfall – the downfall of the Persian king – it is hard to imagine that his losses evoked much sympathy from the Athenian audience.

Rather than focusing on what tragedy is, let us examine what tragedy does. Why did the Athenians invest so much time and effort in staging these works? Poorer citizens were even given an allowance to ensure that they could attend the theatre. This allowance was deemed so important that a law was passed in the fourth century BC that threatened to punish with death any person who proposed to use this fund for purposes other than theatrical subsidy. The tragedies of the fifth century BC clearly mattered to Athens. In the 380s BC, we see a law passed requiring the annual revival of plays by the three great Athenian playwrights Aeschylus (c. 525–456/5 BC), Sophocles (c. 496–406/6 BC), and Euripides (c. 485–407/6 BC).

The Athenians invested so heavily in drama for a number of reasons. First, as we have seen, drama served an important religious purpose. Greeks may have joked that these elaborate performances had 'nothing to do with Dionysus', but in their hearts they knew that this was not true. The processions, sacrifices and choral songs all made sure that Dionysus was prominent in this festival. Second, the Great Dionysia was a festival that bound the community together and raised the imperial profile of Athens. Allies from all over the Empire attended the festival and, together with citizens, resident foreigners and Athenian colonists, they swelled the numbers that marched in the Dionysiac procession. The tribute that Athens demanded from her allies was collected around the time of the festival and displayed in the theatre so that citizens could see the wealth that the Empire brought them. War orphans (children who had lost a father in battle) were paraded in their state-sponsored armour. This was a festival that left no doubt about the might and power of Athens. Finally, it was a festival that taught you something. Through the plays, we see drama inculcating civic virtues in the audience – and at the same time unsettling them, making them less comfortable about the unquestioned assumptions by which they ordered their lives. As Aristophanes remarks, 'We have schoolmasters for little boys; we have poets for grown men.'

The lessons that tragedy taught were varied. As befits its religious context, respect for the Gods was an important theme in the plays. For example, in Euripides' *Hippolytus* (produced 428 BC), the play's title character pours scorn on the goddess Aphrodite. Hippolytus wants nothing to do with the goddess, women or love. Such presumption cannot be tolerated, and so the young prince is brought to ruin on the tragic stage. The goddess fires the passion of his stepmother, Phaedra. Sick with love for her stepson, Phaedra confesses her passion to her nurse who, in turn, informs Hippolytus. Revolted by his stepmother's advances, Hippolytus rejects her, but is unable to tell anyone because the nurse made him swear a solemn oath to keep whatever she told him secret. Ashamed and worried about being exposed, Phaedra commits suicide, but as one final act of revenge she leaves a note accusing her stepson of rape. When her husband Theseus finds the note, he is furious and confronts his son. Still bound by his oath, Hippolytus is unable to explain the situation to his father. Consumed by anger, Theseus curses Hippolytus. Poseidon sends a sea monster that scares the horses of Hippolytus' chariot. In a gruesome death, the chariot falls apart and Hippolytus is caught up in the reins and dragged, fatally, for many miles. And so Aphrodite takes her revenge on the man who dared slight her.

The plays also deal with more human problems and issues of civic politics. As befits an entertainment for the democratic city, tragedy takes a strong stand against tyrants and figures who act tyrannically. Oedipus in Sophocles' play *Oedipus Tyrannus* ('Oedipus, the tyrant') suffers his fate not so much because of the prophecy that he was destined to kill his father and sleep with his mother, rather because he behaves with all the arrogance of a tyrant. Had he been more humble and more approachable, especially when the blind prophet tried to disclose his fate, then many of the worst consequences could have been avoided. In Sophocles' *Antigone*, Cleon (Oedipus' successor at Thebes) has his life ruined because of his tyrannical inflexibility. Unable to compromise when confronted by Antigone's decision to break the law and bury her traitorous brother, Cleon sets off a chain of events that will lead to the death of his son and the suicide of his wife.

Good figures are always recognizable by their espousal of democratic language and slogans. Democratic politics could even cause the dramatists substantially to rework their mythic subject matter. For example, we have a number of myths that show Theseus as a wild, wilful, headstrong king – a model of tyranny. However, on the tragic stage he is transformed. In Euripides' *Suppliants* he becomes the very archetype of the democratic ruler. He is bound by law and consults widely. When challenged by a herald to name the ruler of the land, Theseus responds, 'There is no "ruler" here. This city is without such men. It is ruled by the citizens themselves, rich and poor alike and it is they who take turns to hold the various magistracies. Rich and poor are equal here.'

As we can see, there are moments where the heavy hand of Athenian ideology is on display in Greek tragedy. But it would be a mistake to regard Greek drama as just another form of state propaganda. Drama challenged the preconceptions of the audience as much as it confirmed them. Part of the tension in tragedy is supplied by the way that these plays overturn our comfortable assumptions. Tragedy is the enemy of slogans. For example, many Greeks thought that it was perfectly acceptable to live by the principle of 'helping your friends and harming your enemies'. Tragedy takes this maxim and shows just what a world thus governed would look like. In Euripides' *Trojan Women* (415 BC), we see Troy in the aftermath of the Greek victory. The picture it paints of revenge and recrimination is a terrible one. Once-noble women are parcelled out to cruel or indifferent masters. An innocent child is hurled from the battlements lest he grow up seeking revenge for his murdered father. Never has victory looked so inglorious. In Aeschylus' *Oresteia* trilogy of plays, similar principles lead to a cycle of revenge from which escape seems impossible. Agamemnon slays his daughter Iphigenia. Clytemnestra slays her husband Agamemnon. Orestes slays his mother Clytemnestra. Only divine intervention on the part of Athena can stop this bloodshed. Tragedy demonstrates exactly what is at stake when our lives remain unexamined.

▶ Comedy and satyr-play

It was not just tragedy that could be subversive. Few genres took as much delight in ridiculing contemporary mores as ancient comedy. On the comic stage, everybody was fair game. The more powerful and respected you were, the more likely you were to be subjected to vicious attack. Almost nothing was exempt from the comic wit, and jokes crossed boundaries in a manner that today we would find offensive. The politician Pericles is ruthlessly mocked for the birth defect that gave him an elongated

▲ Actors dressing as satyrs. Red-figure bell krater attributed to the Tarporley painter. 410–380 BC. (Nicholson Museum, Sydney)

head. Another politician is ridiculed for his speech impediment.

We see a similar subversive streak in satyr-play, the other non-tragic genre of drama produced at the Great Dionysia. Sadly, while we have 11 complete Athenian comedies, we have only one near-complete example of a satyr-play. However, we do have a number of fragments of plays and some contemporary discussion of them, so we can reconstruct the genre with reasonable certainty. Unlike the comedies which had independent comic playwrights, satyr-plays were composed by the tragic poets as part of the four plays that they were commissioned to write for the festival. As such, the satyr-play forms a riotous, obscene coda to the serious tragic productions that precede it. As the name suggests, these plays involve the grotesque, mischievous attendants of Dionysus, the part-animal, part-man satyrs. The plots of these plays normally involve parodies of mythological subject matter where well-known stories are turned on their head by the introduction of these foul creatures.

The surviving satyr-play, *Cyclops*, attributed to Euripides, is typical in this respect. The play retells the story of the blinding of the monstrous one-eyed Cyclops by Odysseus. The story was made famous by Homer's *Odyssey* where it features as one of the trials that Odysseus endures as he struggles to make it home from the Trojan War. In this version, Odysseus is washed up on Sicily where he encounters a band of satyrs and their leader, Silenus, who have been separated from the God Dionysus and enslaved by the terrible belching, farting, giant Cyclops. Odysseus brings with him wine and this proves the catalyst for a sequence of calamitous events. Desperate to get the wine, the satyrs trick Odysseus into stealing the Cyclops' food. When this is discovered, Odysseus and his men are attacked and a number killed. The Cyclops and Silenus get drunk, and fuelled by booze and lust the Cyclops abducts Silenus in order to slake his desires. Meanwhile, Odysseus resolves to blind the Cyclops and recruits the satyrs to assist in the plan. This proves a mistake: the cowardly satyrs are not up to the task and come up with increasingly pathetic excuses about why they cannot help. Eventually, Odysseus abandons any hope of using them and relies instead on his crew members. Together the men accomplish the task, the satyrs standing on the sidelines cheering them on. The play ends with Odysseus sailing off and the satyrs cavorting in freedom, planning to return to rejoin Dionysus and his merry band.

Like satyr-plays, ancient Greek comedy delighted in the crude and the grotesque. Jokes about flatulence, excrement and sex acts abound. However, unlike satyr-play, comedy also aimed to offer direct social critique. The humour of comedy was much more pointed. For example, the comic poet might ridicule the justice system or parody trends in contemporary education. Politicians were always fair game. Indeed, ancient comedy is one of our best sources for fifth century political elites. Few prominent individuals seem to have escaped the barbed tongue of the comic poet. Characters mentioned in comedy give us a 'Who's Who' of ancient Athens.

As one would expect, given its prominence in the fifth century BC, the Peloponnesian War features in a number of plays, especially those by the comic dramatist Aristophanes (c. 450–c. 385 BC). Aristophanes paints a bleak picture of Athens during wartime. The poor, especially the rural poor, suffer while indifferent politicians gorge themselves on riches provided by the opportunities of war. There is little that is noble in this conflict. For a number of critics, Aristophanes' plays present a striking, powerful anti-war message – a dramatic protest against Athenian militarism. Yet, as other critics have pointed out, it is often hard to know how seriously to take these anti-war statements. The heroes of Aristophanes' plays are far from trustworthy. They are often chancing schemers driven by self-interest. Dressed in padded costumes that enhanced their buttocks and bellies, and sporting enlarged phalluses, these actors presented characters that one could not envisage as future statesmen. Furthermore, while Aristophanes is very good at pointing out the problems, the solutions he proposes are farcical. How does Aristophanes propose to stop the war and restore good order to the city? According to the solution in *Frogs*, the best way is to descend into the Underworld and bring back the tragic poet Aeschylus to give advice to the city. Equally impractical is the solution proposed in *Peace*, where the main character decides to fly on a giant dung-beetle to the home of the Gods and bring back the goddess Peace to restore order to the world. In *Lysistrata*, Aristophanes proposes that it is only a sex-strike by the women of Athens and Sparta that will bring these two warring cities to heel. In each case, the solutions Aristophanes proposes are fantastic and impossible. Aristophanes might hate the war, but his plays seem to suggest that there is no viable alternative.

Early comedy is very political. It suits the engaged civic life of imperial Athens. As the Empire wanes, tastes begin to change and new forms of comedy arise. These later comedies (often called 'New Comedy') are much less political. They find humour not in the life of the State, but in the life of the household. There is much fun to be had from watching cunning slaves trick their foolish masters, or love-sick boys triumphing over the opposition of disapproving fathers to win the hand of the girl they love. Because these new comedies were less grounded in the politics of the city, they translated more easily to performances outside of Athens. New Comedy became one of Athens' most important exports, and her leading poet Menander (342/1–c. 291 BC) was justly celebrated and his plays were restaged continually all over the Mediterranean. In addition to being restaged, these plays were also adapted by the Romans and form the basis of Roman comedy. Never without a strong dose of self-delusion, the Greeks liked to think that they taught the Romans how to laugh.

Roman spectacles

'Hail, Caesar, those about to die salute you'

Suetonius, *Life of Claudius* (21.6)

▶ The games of Rome

The Roman calendar was filled with festivals and these festivals could be celebrated in extraordinary ways. At the Fordicidia (15 April), unborn calves were ripped from their mothers' wombs and burnt by the Vestal Virgins so that the ashes could be used for purification. At the Lupercalia (15 February), men donned goatskin loincloths and ran semi-naked around the circuit of the Palatine Hill making obscene gestures and striking women with goatskin whips in order to promote fertility or an easy birth. At the Parilia (21 April), men purified their animals' stalls and leapt over burning bales of straw. Such activities contrasted with the far more sombre Lemuria (9, 11 and 13 May) when Romans made offerings of black beans to placate the spirits of the dead while these ghosts wandered the world at night; or the Parentalia (13–21 February) when relatives would visit the tomb of their ancestors, making sacrifices to please the spirits of their deceased relatives.

Few Roman festivals were as idiosyncratic as the Saturnalia (17–23 December), a festival designed to coincide with winter solstice. Described by the poet Catullus as 'the best of days', the festival was one of the most significant in the calendar. During this festival no public business could be conducted, the law-courts and schools were closed, and it was regarded as sacrilege to commence a war. The festival began with a large public sacrifice at the Temple of Saturn in the Roman Forum. This was followed by a public banquet and many private festivities. Gambling was permitted and small gifts were exchanged. Romans abandoned their togas in favour of loose, colourful garments. Social roles were reversed: slaves were permitted to act as free men and mocked their masters while their masters waited on them.

Examining the Roman festival calendar is an alienating experience. Watching all these antics, the Romans look very foreign. Partly, that is the point. The festival cycle of Rome helps create Roman identity, just as the festivals of Easter, Eid al-Fitr, Hanukkah and Diwali help create a notion of what it means to be respectively Christian, Muslim, Jew or Hindu. To outsiders, these festivals seem inexplicable indeed, they serve to delineate who is inside and outside a community. Festivals are also didactic. They teach you how to act in a community and as a community. The social inversions of the Saturnalia reminded everyone how they were supposed to behave normally, outside of festival time.

While some festivals were clearly celebrated in a highly individualistic and singular fashion, others conformed to a more consistent pattern. A formula developed for festivals that involved processions, sacrifices and public feasts. In addition to these core elements, we see the rise of 'games' as an important part of festival celebrations. Games might form part of festivals to celebrate important gods, such as the important cycle of games in honour of Jupiter, Juno and Minerva held on 4–12 September each year. They might be held to give thanks for important victories, such as the Apollinarian games held in gratitude for Apollo's assistance in helping drive the Carthaginians out of Italy. In addition to public games, there were private games such as the funeral games held by members of a family to commemorate the death of an illustrious or well-regarded person.

Games are traditionally divided into two types, 'stage games' and 'circus games'. As the name suggests, 'stage games' were dramatic performances in the theatre. These included both elevated performances of tragedies and more lowbrow farces. From the time of Augustus, they included mimes and pantomimes where dancers, accompanied by music, would present stories from myth using dance and gesture alone. These performances often included elaborate stage sets and rich costumes, and could include acrobats, tightrope-walking, trained animals and visual illusions. Often these acts offered an erotic undertone. Sometimes the effect on the audience could be electric. We have accounts of audiences so swept up in the performance of a dancer impersonating the madness of Ajax that they too went mad and tore off their clothes in their insanity. During a performance by Pylades, one of the most famous pantomimes, a riot broke out and Augustus was forced to exile the performer from the city in order to re-establish good order.

The 'circus games' initially comprised two- and four-horse chariot races. First held in temporary, makeshift structures, their popularity ensured that they were soon housed in purpose-built hippodromes of increasing complexity and magnificence. The Circus Maximus, the largest hippodrome in Rome, measures 600 metres in length and 150 metres in width. There was seating for over 150,000 spectators. Down the middle of the track ran a central spine with turning posts at each end, making a lap of the circus approximately 1,500 metres. Each race consisted of seven laps of the circus and spectators could keep track of the number of circuits that each chariot had completed by referring to large conical balls (called 'eggs') placed on the spine.

Races began when the magistrate who presided over the games gave a signal, normally by dropping a napkin. The number of chariots in any race varied from four to twelve, and up to 25 races could occur in a day. Drivers stood at the back of the chariots, wrapping the reins about their body. This arrangement allowed the driver to use his entire body weight to pull on the reins, but it also increased the level of danger. In the event of an accident, the charioteer risked being dragged to his death. As compensation, the monetary rewards for a successful charioteer could be substantial.

Horseracing elicited strong passions. People gambled heavily on the outcomes of races. Teams of drivers and chariots were divided into four factions, each allocated a different colour (Blue, Green, White, and Red) and people often showed fanatical allegiance to a particular faction. In a fabulously snobbish letter, the Roman writer Pliny (AD 61–c. 112) pours scorn on these fans, mocking them for their passionate following of a colour irrespective of the skills of the charioteers. Later in imperial history, the factions often took on a political colouring. As the world became increasingly autocratic, these factions allowed people an opportunity to voice their opinions of political reforms or individual emperors. Like modern-day hooligans, circus factions could be difficult to control.

In AD 532, following the arrest of leading members of the Green and Blue circus factions, a riot broke out in Constantinople – much of the centre of the city was destroyed and more than 20,000 people may have died.

From the second century BC, we also see another form of game develop in popularity, the beast hunt, in which men were pitted against wild animals. Even the earliest forms of these games presented quite elaborate spectacles. In one event of 168 BC, 63 African panthers and 40 bears and elephants were killed. In 97 BC, the Roman politician Sulla arranged for 100 lions to be hunted by specially-trained North African spearmen. This was apparently the first time that lions were allowed to roam free inside the arena. Prior to this, they had been fettered. The size of the hunts grew exponentially in the Late Republic as the wealth and territorial expansion of Rome allowed those staging the games to import more and more animals from the farthest regions of the known world. Everybody wanted to offer animals that nobody had seen before. The games sponsored by Scarus in 58 BC featured, for the first time, a hippopotamus and crocodiles. Julius Caesar introduced bull-fights and giraffes to the programme. Augustus was the first to exhibit a rhinoceros and a giant snake (possibly an anaconda). Once it was no longer possible to compete in novelty, the magnitude of the hunt became the important consideration. In the events that celebrated the inauguration of the Colosseum, in AD 80, over 5,000 wild beasts and 4,000 tame animals were killed. In games held by the Emperor Trajan (AD 53–117), over 11,000 animals were slaughtered. The emperor Septimius Severus (AD 145–211) constructed a boat in the middle of the amphitheatre; the boat then collapsed and all the different varieties of animals came rushing out, only to be killed. Such butchery produced a large number of carcasses. At the end of each day this meat was auctioned off to an eager public.

A comparatively late arrival into this mix of public games were gladiatorial contests. Originally, these contests were private games held as part of the funeral rites for distinguished individuals. These displays proved popular, and ambitious politicians soon realized that staging such entertainments was an effective way of increasing one's prestige and popularity. Towards the end of the Republic, politicians could be quite brazen in their opportunistic use of these displays. For example, in 46 BC Julius Caesar staged highly elaborate games in the Roman Forum as a way of yet further increasing his political capital and rewarding those who had supported him in his campaign for a second consulship. The pretext for these games was to honour his daughter Julia who had died in childbirth eight years earlier.

Like chariot races, gladiatorial games were initially held in improvised venues where an area was roped off and temporary seating erected. Town centres and marketplaces were popular places in which to hold such contests. As the importance of these contests grew, sponsors desired more grandiose settings in which to stage their entertainments. Out of this desire grew the Roman amphitheatre, a large oval structure with tiers of seats for spectators arranged around a central arena. According to the Roman architectural writer Vitruvius, the elliptical form of these structures harks back to the oblong nature of the town squares in which these games were initially held. Possibly this is true, but the arrangement has a number of practical benefits. The oval shape offers good sightlines and the curved walls ensure that no action is trapped in a corner. Originally, spectators sat exposed to the elements. Later, retractable canvas awnings were supplied for shelter. Judging by the prominence given to the presence of awnings in some surviving advertisements for games, such shelter seems to have been a popular drawcard. The canvases used to provide shelter for spectators in the Colosseum were so large and elaborate that sailors from the Roman navy were used to operate them.

Augustus, as part of his strategy to control all potential sources of popularity in the State and prevent their use by his rivals, incorporated these previously private events into the calendar of state festivals and placed them under the control of magistrates. Limits were placed on the amount that magistrates could spend. No such limitation applied, however, to events staged by the emperor or the imperial family. The imperial games were often tied to events within the life of the imperial family. For example, they might commemorate the anniversary of an accession, a birthday, or a military victory achieved by the emperor or one of his family members. A typical programme for arena games in the imperial period might begin with beast hunts in the morning. At midday, there would be a break, possibly allowing time for musical entertainments or public executions, and then gladiatorial combat in the afternoon. Occasionally, we even have reports of the amphitheatre being flooded and large naval battles staged.

It is unclear precisely when public executions entered the programmes for the games. Certainly, they imbibed its theatrical spirit. The executions were often far from straightforward. We have a number of accounts where the executions were staged in imitation of ancient myths. So, for example, spectators might see a re-enactment of the death of Actaeon, the hunter destroyed by Artemis (Diana): she turned him into a deer, then allowed his hunting dogs to tear him apart. At the games, Actaeon was played by a condemned criminal dressed in a deer costume – and wild dogs were released into the arena. Female criminals might be forced into a bear costume and hunted to death. This scenario reworked the myth of Callisto's punishment – she was turned into a bear by the Gods. Alternatively, they might recreate the sexual congress that supposedly created the Minotaur, and chain a woman inside a replica heifer so that she could be fatally assaulted by a rampaging bull. Sometimes, these spectacular punishments did not go to plan. We have a terrible story about an execution where the condemned was dressed like Icarus, the winged boy who flew too close to the sun and fell to his death. In this re-enactment, rather than his flight being assisted by wings made of wax and feathers, he was shot out of a catapult. Sadly, those operating the catapult miscalculated and fired him with such force that he hit the opposite wall, splattering the emperor and his retinue with gore.

In many ways, these executions represent a logical extension of the rationale that underpinned gladiatorial combat. Gladiatorial combat was a form of execution. Only rarely were gladiators free men. Normally, they were prisoners of war or criminals condemned to life as a gladiator. Contemporary moralists often paint the gladiator as the worst sort of criminals – arsonists or murderers. Although later on free men could volunteer to become gladiators, the profession retained its low social position and this was enforced with a number of particular legal sanctions. Under legislation passed by Augustus, for example, freed gladiators were forbidden from ever attaining Roman citizenship. In Roman law, the gladiator belonged to a group of individuals (along with actors and prostitutes) who suffered *infamia* (lit. 'without good reputation') and so were subject to a number of legal constraints. They were legally classed as untrustworthy and could neither act as witnesses for legal documents nor hold municipal office.

Yet despite this revulsion, the gladiator also exercised a high degree of fascination for the Roman public. Roman literature, perhaps more in fantasy than reality, regularly portrayed gladiators as the object of sexual desire for Roman women. Graffiti attests to the popularity of individual gladiators and accounts of particularly splendid fights were celebrated by Roman popular culture. Crowds could get carried away by these competitions. In AD 59, a riot broke out in Pompeii following a gladiatorial contest as natives of two rival towns exchanged blows and insults. As a result, the Senate decreed that Pompeii be banned from holding any such games for ten years.

Certainly, a lot of thought went into the 'artistry' of the competitions. Gladiators received considerable training at the gladiatorial schools, and were paired in combat to achieve a more even and interesting outcome. So,

▲ Marble relief commemorating the release from service of two female gladiators, Amazon and Achillia. First–second century AD. (© The Trustees of the British Museum)

for example, a heavily armoured but encumbered gladiator might be paired against a more nimble, but less protected opponent. Specialist weapons such as whips, lassoes and spiked gloves also added interest to the encounters. Their weapons and armour could be stylized versions of the distinctive weaponry of foreign nations. So, for example, the Thraex or 'Thracian' fought in a broad-rimmed helmet that enclosed the entire head, with a stylized griffin on the crest. He was armed with a small shield and a curved Thracian sword. The 'Samnite', named after a stubborn Italian hill tribe defeated by the Romans, wore a plumed helmet and carried a long rectangular shield and a short sword. Other identifiable gladiator types that we regularly see represented are the Murmillo (a heavily armoured gladiator with a stylized fish on his helmet) and the Retiarius (a lightly-armoured gladiator with a trident and a net). Like beast hunts, gladiatorial combat often privileged the exotic and unusual. For example, the emperor Domitian enjoyed staging combat between women and there is other evidence that this was not the only time that women fought in the arena.

▶ The triumph

Roman triumphal festivities celebrating their greatest military victories were comparatively brief, but they lingered in the memory. Even centuries after it was held in 61 BC, writers were still regaling their readers with details of the splendid triumph held in honour of Pompey's defeat of Mithradates, the Hellenistic king who proved one of Rome's most dangerous opponents. These celebrations proved inspirational to later generations of kings, princes and emperors who were looking for models for their own splendid celebrations.

Over 300 triumphs were celebrated in Rome's 1,000-year history. Yet despite these numerous occurrences and quite detailed descriptions of these events, much remains unclear about this Roman institution. Take, for example, those monuments that we call 'triumphal arches'. In fact, their connection with the ceremony is not nearly as close as many imagine. A number of arches did commemorate a triumph and would have included a statue on top representing the victorious commander in his four-horse chariot. Berlin's Brandenburg Gate is a fanciful reconstruction of just such an arch. However, many arches have only a slight or tangential relationship with specific triumphs. Napoleon imagined the Roman army processing through them as part of a triumphal parade. This belief seems to be a product of antiquarian confusion whereby these arches were confused with the 'triumphal gate', the gate by which the triumphant general entered the city. As Napoleon's own 30-years-in-the-making Arc de Triomphe showed, getting these structures ready in time for such a parade would have been impossible.

The Roman triumph looks a lot less solid, the more you interrogate it. Some elements are only attested in dubious or contradictory sources. What of the popular image of the slave who stood behind the general holding a crown above his head and whispering in his ear that he needed to remember his mortality? This is the product of putting a lot of weight on a late polemical anti-triumph Christian source. In reality, we do not know whether it was prescribed, common or unusual to have an attendant. Sometimes one appears in the visual depictions of the triumph. At other times, he is absent. It is not even clear if the figure is always a slave. Sometimes sources mention that the attendant would give advice to the general (the wording of the advice is not consistent). In other accounts, he seems to be silent. The rules for the triumph seem rather more variable than traditional accounts imply.

The same goes for the technical requirements of the award of a triumph. According to one version of 'triumphal law', there were a number of criteria to be met before the Senate would award a triumph. These included that the general should hold the office of dictator, consul or praetor, and that he should be holding the office when both the victory was gained and the triumph celebrated. Additionally, 5,000 of the enemy must be slain, the war must be against foreign foes (not a civil conflict), and the war should lead to the dominion of Rome being extended (thus ruling out the recapture of previously controlled territory). Finally, the region in conflict was to have been reduced to an entirely peaceful state. In practice, almost none of these requirements seems absolutely essential to the award of a triumph. We find examples where each of these criteria is ignored. Instead, the award of a triumph seems to have been the result of negotiations and hard lobbying on behalf of the general and his supporters in the Senate. An application for a triumph might be dismissed on a technicality, but this was more the result of a political failure on the part of the general than a legal one. Even the approval of the Senate was not absolutely necessary to the celebration of a triumph. In one infamous case, in 143 BC, we find the general Appius Claudius Pulcher celebrating a triumph without even obtaining the permission of the Senate.

Once permission was granted to hold a triumph, preparations could begin for the festivities. The centrepiece of the triumph, which also included feasts, sacrifices and even sometimes attendant games, was the triumphal procession. The victorious general was granted permission to enter the city of Rome with his army (almost the only time that a general was so allowed) and process to the Temple of Jupiter Optimus Maximus ('Jupiter Best and Greatest') on the Capitoline Hill to make sacrifices on behalf of the city.

The challenge for the general was to make the procession as impressive as possible. This was his best opportunity to establish and cement the public perception of his achievements. Those who could afford it certainly spared no expense. We have accounts of tremendous trains of captured war-booty including jewels, bullion, works of art, exotic animals and plants (sometimes whole forests of trees), and libraries of literature. The more distinctive and precious the object the better. The Arch of Titus, whose panels includes reliefs of the emperor's triumph after the defeat of Jerusalem, gives great prominence to the large gold menorah that featured in his parade. Painted panels held up by soldiers and attendants announced specific achievements and glorified the defeat of illustrious opponents. In Julius Caesar's triumph, naturally one of the placards read 'Veni, Vidi, Vici' ('I came, I saw, I conquered'). Captives (sometimes chained, sometimes not) were paraded before the populace to the jeers of the crowd. Numbers of captives varied. In one account (probably unreliable) 8,000 captives are mentioned. In another, poor Gnaeus Octavius had no captives to parade after his naval victory. More important than number were the high status individuals captured: foreign kings, leader, generals, and their families were the real prize. Seeing the proud humbled emphasized the magnitude of the Roman victory. For this reason, a number of foreign rulers refused to participate. Both Cleopatra and Mithradates committed suicide instead of giving their opponents the pleasure of parading them in a triumph. Behind the captives came the victorious general in his four-horse chariot. Again, the emphasis was on spectacle: if he could afford it, the chariot might be studded with jewels. The horses would be the finest available. Pompey even tried to have his chariot pulled by four elephants instead of horses, but had to abandon this plan when the chariot got caught in a gateway.

Julius Caesar had a similar upset in his triumph when his chariot broke its axle (inauspiciously outside the Temple of Fortune) and he was almost thrown out. Perhaps the hardest element of the procession to stage-manage were the soldiers that followed the general. Crowned like their general in laurel wreaths, these soldiers were often prone to misbehaviour. Their antics could border on the obscene. In Julius Caesar's triumph in 46 BC, the soldiers took great pleasure in singing songs that mocked the hero for his supposed passive homosexuality ('Caesar screwed the lands of Gaul, Nicomedes screwed our Caesar') and his fondness for seducing married women ('Romans, watch your wives, the bald adulterer is back'). In a festival centred around the cult of one man, the actions of the soldiers look like a small act of resistance – a reminder to the powerful that the glories they enjoyed came at the expense of the sweat and blood of the Roman soldiery.

Material culture

*'Neither talent without instruction,
nor instruction without talent can
produce the perfect craftsman.'*

Vitruvius, Roman architect and engineer (c.70–25 BC)

Among the many fans of ancient ingenuity and design is Barack Obama. In 2010, the US President used his considerable influence to arrange for the team behind the popular science television programme *Mythbusters* to devote a section of their show to the solar death-ray designed by the Greek intellectual Archimedes (c. 287–212 BC). Obama was very keen to see this machine in action and was desperate for them to prove that it was not a myth.

The evidence from our ancient sources about this miraculous invention is meagre. No account gives the complete story. From tantalizing scraps of information, a standard account has emerged which has Archimedes developing a fabulous device that used mirrors to focus the sun's rays and set fire to the invading Roman fleet during the siege of Syracuse (214–212 BC). The weapon was extremely successful, supposedly destroying a number of enemy ships. In some later versions of the story, it was this weapon that caused the Romans to make the capture of Archimedes a priority and caused one over-eager Roman soldier to kill the scientist.

Like many of the stories about the ancient world, this account does not stand up to too much scrutiny. Many of the key elements are suspect. For example, it is not clear that the initial version of the story even featured mirrors. It may well have been referring to catapults that threw fiery combustible material onto the ships, rather than mirrors. Even the accounts that feature mirrors are inconsistent. We do not know whether Archimedes' device consisted of one mirror or many mirrors. We do not even know whether the fires that broke out on the ships were deliberately intended by Archimedes or the by-product of his attempt to use mirrors to blind the sailors, and so make them vulnerable to attack.

Yet despite all these uncertainties, the image of Archimedes and his primitive laser has been a potent one ever since late antiquity. President Obama is part of a long tradition of scholars, enthusiasts and rulers who have wanted to see this invention in action. It is a popular story. When the *Mythbusters* team had previously investigated this weapon (in 2004 and 2006), they had declared that the contraption could never work. However, viewers were not prepared to accept this verdict. Almost immediately a campaign began to reopen the case with President Obama among its most high-profile supporters. Students at MIT staged their own reconstruction to show that with the right number of mirrors and the right climatic conditions, a large group of tightly focused mirrors could scorch the wooden deck of a ship. On 8 December 2010 this lobby group obtained its wish and the case was revisited on TV. Sadly, once again it proved impossible to recreate Archimedes' weapon in any usable form and it was declared a 'myth'. No matter how many mirrors one uses and no matter what the conditions, a workable form of weapon is impossible to create.

In many ways, Archimedes' death-ray is symbolic of much ancient technology. We have lots of stories about fabulous machines – steam-powered birds that flew through the air, water-powered organs, and automatic door-openers. Ancient technology always sounds very grand and appears to have such great potential. However, in reality, the existence and practical usefulness of much of this ancient complex machinery is debatable. Such technological marvels that we can recover, such as the extraordinary Antikythera mechanism used to calculate the movement of planets, never saw widespread adoption. On the whole, the existence of these machines is more anecdotal than real. They generate a lot of commentary – we know of three ancient works devoted either entirely or in large part to the topic of 'burning mirrors', for example – but ancient technology was always the stuff of toys rather than engines for dynamic, industrial change.

This does not mean that the ancient world was unable to produce works of outstanding sophistication. There is a reason why the origin of so many modern museums lies in collections of Greek and Roman antiquities. Through their use of imagery, the care taken in their manufacture, and the enormous resources deployed in their construction, the art and architecture of the classical world are prized for good reason.

▶ The foreign origins of art

We always need to remember that the Greeks and Romans are Mediterranean peoples. As such, they exist as part of a much larger network of cultures that includes the Near East, Egypt and North Africa. As much older and more developed cultures, these neighbours had a profound influence on the comparatively younger states. It is easy to see the mark of Egypt, for example, on ancient Greek statuary and architecture. The stiff, angular forms of the early Greek statues called *kouroi*, clearly borrow from Egyptian prototypes. Similarly, it is hard not to see the acanthus-leaved capitals of Corinthian columns as harking back to the vegetative columns that adorn so many Egyptian temples. Some scholars have even claimed that everything worthwhile in Greek culture is borrowed from Egypt. This is clearly an overstatement. While we should never forget the tremendous debt that the classical world owes to the nations that surrounded it, we also should not ignore the tremendous changes that the Greeks and Romans wrought and the extent to which they adapted their source material to make it their own.

▲ Oedipus and the Sphinx. Detail from Hellenistic sarcophagus. National Archaeological Museum, Athens. (© Ancient Art & Architecture Collection Ltd/Alamy)

Take, for example, a creature like the sphinx. These creatures with a human head placed on an animal's body are found in a number of cultures. There are Persian sphinxes, Assyrian sphinxes and Egyptian sphinxes. The Greek sphinx owes its origins to these foreign models. Yet, the Greek sphinx is not just a carbon copy. It is a very distinct beast. One important difference is gender. Greek sphinxes are normally female. Most Near Eastern and Egyptian sphinxes are male. The Greek sphinx also exists within a nest of stories and associations that makes it unique. The Egyptian sphinx is a guardian, a sign of royal power. The Greek sphinx is the opposite. She is a disruptive influence. She tests people with riddles, killing them should they fail to answer. It took a hero like Oedipus to answer her most famous riddle: 'What creature is a biped, a triped and a quadruped?' (Answer: Man, he crawls on all fours when he is a baby, walks on two feet as a man, and stumbles about with the aid of a staff in old age).

In the way in which the Greeks domesticated the sphinx, we can see how even the most foreign elements can be incorporated and reinvented in classical culture. These borrowings start at the very beginning of Greek and Roman civilization and never really stop. The Greeks and Romans were great adopters. There was always a ready market for foreign goods and when foreign goods could not be obtained in the right quantity, we see local craftsmen moving in to produce pleasing imitations. It is this permeability that was one of the great strengths of classical culture.

Certain features particularly distinguish classical art from its foreign rivals. The first is the priority given to naturalism. For various reasons, the Greeks decided that beauty resided in nature. It proved to be a crucial decision. Classical art was a competitive business. We possess numerous stories of rival artists vying to outdo each other. One famous anecdote concerns two rival painters, Zeuxis and Parrhasios. Each is charged to produce their finest work. Zeuxis unveils his depiction of grapes so remarkably life-like that a flock of passing birds swoops down and starts to peck at the grapes. Zeuxis is instantly filled with pride. What better sign could there be of skill than this? Quietly confident, he turns to Parrhasios and asks him to pull back the curtain and unveil his picture. At which point, Parrhasios reveals that the curtain is his painting. Fooled into believing that the painted canvas was actually a real curtain, Zeuxis instantly concedes the victory to Parrhasios because, as he says, 'I managed to paint something which fooled animals, you've painted something which has fooled a man'. This story is almost certainly invented, but it illustrates two important features about classical art. It highlights its competitive nature and shows how that competition was often based around a contest in realism; to perfectly imitate nature was the goal of the ancient artist.

We see this most obviously in sculpture of the body. As we have seen, the earliest Greek statues resemble in the stiffness of their pose and their schematic anatomy examples from Egypt and the Near East. Although even here, at the point where the artistic traditions are closest, there are significant differences. For one thing, the Greek statue is naked. This preference for naked display is marked. No other culture in the

Mediterranean shares it and the Greeks were proud to regard it as a distinguishing feature of their culture. Even the Romans who admired the Greeks in so much of their cultural output balked at the adoption of nudity. Eventually they succumbed, but it was only after some resistance. The rise of the nude statue in Rome is a comparatively late feature.

From these early statues, we see the figures becoming increasingly refined. The bodies loosen and the poses become more natural. The anatomy of the figures becomes more complex and articulated. The bodies start to come alive, assuming poses of such fluidity that they are practically impossible for normal human beings to achieve. This realism becomes even more marked when we remember that these statues would not have been white marble, but painted to resemble human flesh.

Sometimes realism was even pursued at the expense of beauty. In the fifth and fourth centuries BC, we see a preference in sculpture for a very distinct, but ultimately unreal, body type. On the whole, as befits their athletic and divine subject matter, the figures are young, fit and attractive. Even more mature males, such as the older Gods, are shown in robust health. However, later on, in the Hellenistic period we start to notice changes. There is still a market for the young and beautiful, but these body types start to be joined by older and more haggard bodies. Realism triumphs, even over attractiveness.

This was sentiment to which the Romans could relate. Their culture had a distinctive distrust of the too-beautiful body. For the Roman man, it was the body scarred in the service of the state that was beautiful. The old body was the mature, sensible, serious, respectable body. For these reasons, we notice a distinct trend in Roman art for what is termed 'veristic art', a style that privileges realism over cosmetic flattery. We see it expressed most obviously in that distinctive Roman artistic product, the portrait bust. Here every wrinkle is emphasized, every scar noted and wound highlighted. Here realism evokes not beauty, but authority.

A fetishization of the natural, especially the body, is one of the most the distinctive features of classical art. A second feature that is particularly noticeable about classical art is its fondness for narrative. As art developed, decoration quickly gave way to storytelling. We see this in the sculptures that decorate temples. Early temples often fill their pediments with large, impressive, often frightening creatures. These monsters lurking in the rooftops create an appropriate sense of religious awe. However, they do not have a story to tell and it was narrative that the Ancients came to prize in their art. As a result, we see temple pediments change. Large monstrous beasts give way to figures depicting mythological scenes. So, for example, while the pediments of the early temples in Athens might show monstrous snaky creatures, by the time the Parthenon is built in the fifth century BC, these creatures are replaced with scenes showing the Birth of Athena and the Contest between Athena and Poseidon for control of Athens. Contrary to the impression given in most modern museums, classical art did not want its viewers to stare at it in silence – it wanted to be the start of a conversation. It wanted to be talked about.

▶ Ode on a Grecian urn

Walk into any collection of classical antiquities and you are bound to encounter Greek vases. Apart from coins, no object survives from ancient Greece in such large quantities as painted pottery. Unlike metal or marble, pottery was never melted down or crushed up for building materials. It is hard to destroy. Vases may crack, but the individual pieces remain. Walk the Greek landscape and you will often stumble upon fragments of ancient pots. No archaeological excavation could proceed without its pottery expert. Dig anywhere and you will almost always discover ceramics.

It can be rather intimidating to see shelf after shelf of Greek vases. This is partly the fault of museums that treat vases (never called 'pots') as if they were prestige art objects. Like cherished masterpieces, they catalogue them according to their style of decoration (e.g. black-figure, red-figure) and attribute them to individual artists (e.g. the Brygos painter). While this connoisseurship is valuable for scholars, it often stands in the way of being able to truly appreciate these vases as objects in their own right. The Ancients would have found the care that we lavish on these vases extraordinary. After all, compared to the gold and silver drinking vessels that we know existed, pottery drinking vessels are comparatively common. They were not art objects. These were objects that were meant to be used and they need to be put back into their original context before they can come alive.

The vast majority of Greek vases that you see on display in museums were designed for one particular function, the Greek drinking party known as the 'symposium' (lit. 'drinking together'). A lot of these vases were produced in Athens and many were exported to places like Italy where they often formed part of the goods buried with the deceased. Indeed, most of our best-preserved Athenian vases come from tombs. Yet, while they clearly served an important function in the afterlife, it was for daily life they were designed, and the symposium in particular. Symposia were largely all-male occasions (there were occasionally flute girls) and they were the bedrock of Greek social life. Guests would recline on couches, sing songs, play games and engage in witty repartee.

They would also drink. And for the Greeks, drinking was a serious business. It was governed by elaborate rules and it required extensive paraphernalia. It is the complex requirements of Greek drinking practice that explain the large variety of shapes that survive. For us, drinking wine is a relatively straightforward process. We open a bottle of wine and pour it into a glass. Not so for the Greeks. The Greeks never drank wine straight. It was always mixed with water. Drinking unmixed wine was a sign of barbarism, the sort of thing that you might expect from an uncultured foreigner or an uncivilized monster like a boisterous centaur. The ideal proportions were a matter of debate, but a ratio of 1:3 (wine to water) was fairly standard. In order to dilute the wine, the wine was poured from the amphora in which it was stored into a large mixing-bowl, called a *krater*. Water was then poured into the krater from a three-handled jug, called a *hydria*. Once the wine and water were mixed, it was ladled out into individual drinking cups (such as the large flat cup called a *kylix*) and served to guests.

It was the elaborate rules of the symposium that governed the imagery we find on Greek vases. Vase painters often liked to play with the ritual of the symposium in the decoration. So, for example, one painter might paint a flotilla of ships on the inside lip of a krater, so that when it was filled it looked like the ships were sailing on the sea (the fact that Homer describes the sea as 'wine dark' just adding potency to the imagery).

Much fun was had with drinking cups. As the cup was handed to the guest already full of wine, he had no idea what image might lurk on the bottom of the cup. The fact that this part of the cup, known as the *tondo*, was initially concealed by wine encouraged the artist to play with the imagery. Sometimes they might paint a Gorgon's face, so that as the drinker drained his cup, he suddenly found himself staring straight into the eyes of a petrifying monster. At other times, they might paint an explicit pornographic scene to shock and surprise the drinker.

As well as being decorative, the images on vases could be didactic. Sometimes, it was a general didacticism. So scenes of martial valour or civic life might be held up as examples of ideal behaviour. At other times, the messages were quite pointed. There are a number of vases that warn about the dangers of over-indulgence at the symposium. So, for example, a number of vomiting scenes or hangover scenes can be found in the bottom of cups – reminders to the drinker about the consequences of having one too many. Comic satyrs painted on vases often served a similar purpose. Their grotesque antics showed the inverse of how a sensible person should behave.

Seen through the lens of the symposium, the oddities and peculiarities of Greek vases suddenly become explicable. Whenever you encounter one, you just need to put yourself back into the context of a Greek drinking party and think about how this vase would have been used.

▶ Roman wall-painting

Just as Greece has become synonymous with black-and-red painted pottery, so too has Rome become associated with the rich, painted rooms of its villas and houses. While the survival of robust, hard-wearing pottery is not surprising, the fact that we know so much about these delicate painted walls is remarkable. It is largely due to one spectacular, cataclysmic event.

On 24 August AD 79, Mount Vesuvius violently exploded sending up great clouds of ash and pumice into the sky. The debris blanketed the area. The citizens of the nearby towns of Pompeii and Herculaneum huddled indoors sheltering from the explosion. This was to prove a fatal mistake. At some point on the following day, great outpourings of hot gas and rock (not lava) erupted from the sides of the volcano. Called pyroclastic flows, these eruptions proved fatal to the citizens of the nearby towns. With tremendous force, these super-hot flows flattened structures, incinerating and suffocating the population. Close to 16,000 citizens died in the eruption, the vast majority of them as a result of the pyroclastic flows.

While the flows proved fatal for the citizens of these towns, they proved a boon for archaeologists. The heat carbonized much of the wood and the layers of ash and pumice preserved other material. The destruction had proved so total that the sites of habitation were abandoned and there was no substantial attempt to rebuild there. The sites remained largely undisturbed until the eighteenth century, when workmen stumbled upon the remains of Herculaneum. Subsequent excavation of the surrounding area a decade later uncovered the town of Pompeii.

The sites were immediately recognized for their importance and for the quality of the goods that they produced. Previously, substantial finds had largely been the product of excavating burials. Pompeii and Herculaneum were unique in producing large quantities of material from an actual domestic context. From jewellery to children's cribs, every conceivable kind of good emerged from the sites, most in a high state of preservation. It was even possible to reconstruct the bodies of the deceased. Noticing that voids in the ash often contained bones, excavators developed a technique of pouring plaster into the voids so that the forms of the victims could be reconstructed. Men, women, children and even dogs have been recovered in this way.

Pompeii produced many treasures, but among the most valuable of them must be the high quality plaster wall-paintings that decorated the houses of the wealthy. So extensive were the finds that they allowed historians to understand and catalogue the development of the art form. Traditionally, Roman wall-painting is divided into four styles. In the earliest style, the First Style, the walls are painted to simulate expensive finishes such as marble or alabaster. The Second Style extends this by adding architecture elements such as columns as well as painted panels that contain trompe l'oeil features. The illusionism of the Second Style is further developed by the Third Style, which adds more figures and more colourful decoration. The architectural features tend to be more linear and delicate. The final style, the Fourth Style, while less ornamented than the Third, introduces large-scale narrative paintings into the mix as well as illusionistic panoramic vistas.

Within this broad schema, it was possible to achieve tremendous variety in terms of subject matter and subsidiary decoration. Juxtaposing images allowed artists and their patrons to play clever games. Take, for example, one room from a well-known house in Pompeii, the House of the Vettii. This house is famous for the quality of its wall paintings and the decoration is typical of the Fourth Style. A small earthquake in AD 62 seems to have provided the opportunity to redecorate the house in the latest style.

The house is full of paintings. From the well-endowed Priapus weighing his member in the doorway to the amusing cupids hard at work in the main reception room, these paintings have proven as popular with modern-day tourists as they presumably were to the house's original owners. The room I want to discuss can be found off the garden courtyard. In antiquity, it would have been used as a dining and reception room.

The room features a number of large painted panels depicting mythological scenes. Individually, each of the scenes is of high quality. They may even be imitations of now-lost masterpieces. However, what is striking is the effect produced when these images are assembled together. The Romans were masters of the juxtaposition. They were exemplary copyists. Most of the sculptures that we think of as Greek sculpture today are actually Roman copies of Greek originals. Yet, it would be a mistake to see them as just copyists. They were skilled manipulators of images. Through the juxtaposition of pre-existing imagery, it was possible to create new meaning. The paintings in this reception room provide a good example of this.

We know that part of the enjoyment that the Romans derived from paintings was the opportunity they provided for viewers to display their learning and culture by spotting allusions, adding additional contexts and creating connections between the works. On a basic level, all the paintings in this room allude to a common geographic location. They all show myths depicting Thebes, just as all the paintings in another reception room show myths connected with Crete. However, the themes that connect the paintings in this room go beyond place. One of the issues that the paintings address is the revelation of divinity – what happens when Gods enter the scene. The picture they paint is not a pretty one.

The central panel on the wall facing you as you enter the room depicts the death of Pentheus. The young man kneels, surrounded by maenads, the followers of the god Dionysus, who are about to rend him limb from limb. One maenad stands above him, ready to dash his brains out with a rock. Another leaps from a rock to stick him with her ivy-garlanded spear. It is a violent, unpleasant scene. Pentheus' crime? Not to recognize the god Dionysus when he returned to Thebes. Foolishly, Pentheus declared the God a charlatan and for this he paid a terrible price. We see the consequences of making a similar mistake on the right-hand wall. This painting depicts a similarly dreadful demise, this time the brutal death of Dirce. In the painting, we see her twin nephews engineering her murder. They tie her hair to the horns of a bull that will trample her to death. Again, the mistake that Dirce made was not to recognize the arrival of the divine. When her niece Antiope claimed that Jupiter had appeared before her and that they had subsequently enjoyed sexual intercourse, Dirce refused to accept her story, believing instead that Antiope had made the story up as a cover for an illicit love affair. She tormented Antiope and when Antiope subsequently fell pregnant she arranged for the children to be exposed. In the painted panel, we see these children now full grown, reunited with their mother, and exacting an exquisite vengeance on her persecutor. The final image in the room seems innocent in comparison. It shows the family of the infant Hercules looking on in amazement as he strangles snakes that have been sent to kill him. It is a well-known story from Hercules' childhood and judging from the number of versions around Pompeii, it seems to have been a popular story. Yet here, flanked by these other images, the story takes on a darker countenance. There is an unpleasant thread running through this story. The killing of the snakes might announce the arrival of Hercules on the scene, but for his family it also means confronting some unpleasant truths. The father, Amphitryon, is forced to acknowledge that his son is not his child, but the offspring of Jupiter. His wife, Alcmene, now realizes that she has incurred the wrath of the wife of Jupiter, Juno, who clearly wants to kill the boy. Tragedy lurks behind this scene of triumph.

An analysis of the images in this room demonstrates that Roman wall-painting was not just decorative. It was clever, designed to get the viewer to think. Whether it was about the content of myth, the pleasures of the garden or the nature of perception, paintings played with and often confounded your expectations. Like all ancient art, it challenged the viewer to explain the image. It certainly was not Roman wallpaper.

▶ Marvels of architecture and engineering

Size mattered in the ancient world. Generally speaking, the Ancients thought that bigger was best. Greek heroes were larger than life-sized. The Gods are routinely depicted as larger than man. Given this propensity for gigantism, it should not surprise us to see a similar aesthetic operating in ancient building works. We see this most clearly in that list of the most impressive structures in antiquity, the 'Seven Wonders of the Ancient World'. Making lists was a popular pastime in antiquity and numerous lists of wonders circulated. The most influential one is preserved in a poem by the second century BC poet Antipater of Sidon. In the traditional list, the Seven Wonders include:

1 The Great Pyramid at Giza

2 The Hanging Gardens of Babylon

3 The Temple of Artemis at Ephesus

4 The Statue of Zeus at Olympia

5 The Mausoleum of Halicarnassus

6 The Colossus of Rhodes

7 The Lighthouse of Alexandria

When trying to determine how each of these structures made it onto the list, it is hard to overlook size as an important determinant. Few visitors to Egypt are not impressed by the monumentality of the Great Pyramid. In its day, the temple of Artemis at Ephesus was the largest temple of its type. Size seems to have been part of the reason why it is the statue of Zeus at Olympia on the list and not the statue of Athena from the Parthenon. Both were large, impressive chryselephantine ('gold-and-ivory') statues designed by the same artist, Phidias. However, the statue of the Zeus was the larger and certainly left visitors with an impression of its bulk. In contrast, the statue of Athena seems much more appropriate to the scale of the Parthenon. She looks like she could walk out of the main doors, rather than having to burst out of the building.

Athena suits her building and the Parthenon reminds us that it was not just questions of scale that obsessed ancient architects. Other aesthetic issues were at play. It may not have made it onto the list of the 'Seven Wonders', but many scholars are prepared to declare that the Parthenon represents the finest example of Greek architecture. There are a number of reasons for giving the building this accolade. Part of the justification rests on the delicate optical refinements that were introduced into the building. Despite its tremendous scale (the building measures 69.5 m x 30.9 m), gentle curves were introduced into the base of the temple and the columns were carved so that they widen at the bottom. This was done in order to counteract the distorting effect of vision whereby parallel lines often appear from a distance to bow and sag. By introducing these imperceptible curves, the eye is tricked: the curved lines seem straight and the building looks perfect. It is due to such attention to detail as well as the exquisite quality of its sculptural decorations that the Parthenon is such a favourite with architectural historians.

The omission of the Parthenon from the list of 'Seven Wonders' seems odd. However, even more striking is the fact that the list does not include any Roman works. The list has a distinctly Greek bias. Partly, this is explained by the fact that the list was compiled early, before large-scale Roman building works became famous. Yet, the fact that the list was never updated makes one suspect Greek cultural chauvinism at play. It is a very political act to declare that there is nothing of wonder in the Roman world.

It is also deeply unfair. The Romans were just as proud and active builders as the Greeks. One of the many boasts that Augustus made about his reign was that he 'found a city of bricks and left a city of marble'. They were also more skilled engineers than the Greeks. The invention of concrete as well as the perfection of the arch allowed them to construct buildings that Greeks would have thought impossible. The Greeks built a number of circular buildings, but there is nothing in the Greek world to rival the splendid Pantheon of Rome. Even today, it is still the world's largest unreinforced concrete dome.

Time and again, we see the Romans eclipsing the Greeks in building projects. For example, the Greeks may have been justly proud of the Colossus of Rhodes, but Roman emperors were also fond of erecting huge statues. Perhaps, the best-known imperial Colossus in antiquity was the bronze statue, over 30 metres high, that Nero commissioned to decorate his spectacular palace, the 'Golden House' (Domus Aurea).

The remains of Nero's Golden House still exist. Although all of its opulent fittings have been stripped away, a lot of the decorative detail remains and these extensive ruins give a strong sense of how magnificent the palace must have been in its heyday. Sadly, Nero's Colossus has been completely lost. We know that it was moved by the Emperor Hadrian from the Golden House to stand outside the Flavian Amphitheatre, where it remained until, at least, the fourth century AD. Indeed, the modern name for the amphitheatre, the Colosseum, is derived from the statue. The name 'colosseum' does not refer to the building's enormous size, rather it refers to its location: it is the building next to the Colossus.

Of course, you did not need Nero's Colossus to find your way to the Colosseum. Visit Rome and it is hard to escape this building. The building impresses through its size rather than its architectural ingenuity. When construction began in AD 70 (the building was finally finished a decade later), Rome had been building large amphitheatres for a considerable time and the Colosseum conforms to a fairly traditional design. Still, the scale is impressive. The building measures 188 metres at its longest axis and 156 metres across. It stands 48.5 metres high and had a capacity of between 50,000 and 80,000 spectators. Beneath the wooden floor of the Colosseum was an extensive network of chambers where wild animals were kept and mechanical elevators and machinery for stage effects were stored.

Yet, the Colosseum represents just the tip of a very large iceberg of Roman building practice. Following Augustus, emperors were keen to beautify the capital. Every ruler was eager to leave their mark. This had an important effect outside Rome as well. Regional cities took their cues from Rome and we see regional elites and Roman provincial administrators imitating practices at Rome. If you wanted to count in the Roman world, you needed to leave your name on a building. Teams of talented craftsman toured the Empire disseminating popular styles of decoration as well as new building techniques. Although it is possible to note regional variations in architecture, wall-painting and mosaic design, it is odd, given the size of the Empire, that such variation is not much greater. There was something always intrinsically attractive about the Roman product. From Hadrian's Wall in the UK, to the Pont du Gard in southern France, to Leptis Magna in North Africa, to Bosra in Syria, the Roman building programme has left enduring scars on the landscape. Travel round Europe and you are often travelling on roads and pathways that were first laid down by the Romans. The cities that the Romans created dominated the European imagination for centuries. Paris, Vienna and Berlin have, at various times, each been substantially remodelled according to Roman design precepts. The boundaries of the 'City of London' were established by the Romans and almost all the traditional 'gates' of London (Ludgate, Newgate, etc.) have their origins in the Roman town plan. Even centuries later, our town and cities are still shaped by the Romans.

8

Ancient philosophy

'The unexamined life is not worth living.'

Plato, Greek philosopher (c. 428–348 BC)

▶ Weirdos in beards

It is easy to spot the busts of philosophers in museums. It is the beard that gives them away. Anybody who wanted to be taken seriously as an intellectual in the ancient world needed a beard. Being clean-shaven was reserved for youths and athletes. A face without stubble was a sign of a man of action like Alexander the Great, not a man of contemplation. Indeed, a mature man who liked to shave was regarded as a slightly shady character. The writer Dio Chrysostom (c. AD 40–115) praised the councillors of a Greek city on the Bosphorus for their long flowing beards. 'A philosopher would have been extremely pleased at the sight', he remarked, 'There was only one man who was clean-shaven and as a result he was ridiculed and hated by all.' This man's lack of facial hair was taken as a sign of betrayal of his homeland's intellectual traditions, an attempt to curry favour with the Roman oppressors.

This fixation with facial hair tells us a lot about the status and function of philosophy and philosophers in the ancient world. The first, and most important, is that philosophers were distinctive, recognizable, a breed apart. Philosophy was a practice for separating yourself from the herd. Some took this to extremes. The philosopher, Diogenes, for example, was infamous for his anti-social activities. Many stories were told about his life. He supposedly lived in a giant storage jar in the central marketplace of Athens. Unshaven and unwashed, he rolled his jar onto the hot sands

▲ Marble heads of the philosophers Epicurus, Antisthenes and Socrates; marble bust of the Stoic philosopher Chrysippus. (© The Trustees of the British Museum)

in summer so that he sweltered and in winter he wandered the streets barely clothed and embraced snow-covered statues so that he experienced the pain of bitter cold. No person, no matter what their status, was exempt from his abuse. He wandered the city with a lamp during daylight hours pompously declaring that he was looking unsuccessfully for an honest man. He berated Alexander the Great for standing around and blocking out the sun when he came to visit him. In an insulting lesson to the prince, he pretended to be unable to distinguish the bones of Alexander's father Philip from the bones of a common slave. The point that Diogenes makes about the equality that we all experience in death is a valid one, but it certainly did not need to be put in such outrageous terms. Admittedly, a lot of the stories about Diogenes are no doubt fictitious or exaggerations. However, the impression they leave is the right one. Philosophy was a practice that involved going against the grain. Socrates claimed to be the gadfly that constantly and annoyingly pricked the conscience of the city. Pythagoras demanded strict vegetarianism from his followers and in doing so effectively excluded them from all the major civic occasions as these traditionally involved the sacrifice and consumption of animals.

The second point worth observing is that the identification of philosophy with a 'look' reflects the fact that philosophy was less about specific areas of study than it was about a particular attitude. As we shall see, ancient philosophy encompassed a wide variety of thinking that we would separate out into different disciplines such as science, medicine, ethics and theology. Philosophers were not just teachers, they could also be poets, physicians and mystics. It was not a one-size-fits-all profession.

Finally, it is worth noting that Hellenism and philosophy go hand in hand. Many Romans practised philosophy and Rome produced a number of distinguished philosophers. However, the idea that philosophy was fundamentally a 'Greek' practice remained hard to shake. It is to Greece that one first needs to turn to get the story of philosophy.

▶ The origins of philosophy

The conventional history of Greek philosophy begins in the sixth century BC. It does so for a reason. This was a period in which Greece was undergoing immense changes. Economic and social revolutions were sweeping through the Greek world. Greeks were travelling like they never had before. Colonies were being established all over the Mediterranean. Challenging encounters with new ideas, cultures and customs were inevitable, and out of such tremendous change emerged new ways of thinking.

It is no accident that change was a topic that interested these thinkers. How much does something need to change before it is a completely different object? This was a question that resonated with the time, and a number of figures came forward to offer opinions. Heraclitus put forward the proposition that it was impossible to step into the same river twice. The nature of the river changed as swiftly as its flowing waters. Or did it? Heraclitus actually posed the issue as a paradox. In doing so, he got his audience to think about the nature of identity. The biographer Plutarch tells us that the paradox of the ship of Theseus was much loved by ancient philosophers. In Athens, it was still possible to see the ship in which King Theseus had sailed to Crete to battle the Minotaur. The only problem was that as each board had rotted away, it had, in turn, been replaced. Was it still the same ship? How many boards had to be replaced before it was a new ship? Plutarch tells us that it was possible hear rival camps disputing this question even hundreds of years later.

One of the functions of philosophy was to question accepted certainties. In doing so, philosophers trampled on the prerogatives of a number of other groups. For example, poets such as Hesiod produced standard mythological accounts of how the world came into being. Poets synthesized stories and produced an account of how the universe emerged from chaos, Gods and monsters were created, and the ages of Man developed. These were wonderful stories, but they were riddled with holes and contradictions.

Philosophers offered rival accounts. They attempted to provide a more logically consistent story. Worried about the mechanisms by which change came into the world and the origins of matter, they proposed accounts that privileged certain elements (e.g. water, fire, air, or a mixture of them) or postulated certain forces that manipulated matter and motivated change (e.g. love or strife). Most of their accounts still had a place for Gods – atheism in antiquity was remarkably rare – but their divinities were quite different to the deities of Greek myth. Indeed, encounters with foreign religious beliefs prompted some to question much conventional thinking about the Gods. Xenophanes (c. 570–c. 475 BC), for example, questioned whether Greeks were correct in their depictions of the gods by pointing out that Ethiopian gods were dark and snub-nosed, while the Thracians gods were blue-eyed and red-haired. He even went on to speculate that, 'if cows and horses or lions had hands or could draw with their hands and make artefacts like men – horses would draw the forms of their gods like horses and cows like cows.' Maybe, as Xenophanes hints, man is really behind these gods.

Not even our senses or our logic were immune to philosophic questioning. Profound scepticism is a theme running through a number of philosophic schools. Zeno of Elea (c. 490–430 BC), through a series of famous paradoxes, questioned whether we really know what we claim to know. For example, we all know that arrows fly through the air. However, when Zeno questions you on this point, you might not be so certain. Zeno loved to play with the idea that space and time could be infinitely divided. If you accept these premises, then certain perverse consequences follow. Take, for example, the movement of an arrow. When an arrow travels from point A to point B, does it not have to travel through a mid-point (let us call it C) before it can arrive at B? And if it travels through C, does it not first have to travel between another mid-point (D) that exists between A and C? And if it travels through this mid-point, does it not first have to travel through another mid-point (E)? And so on. And as space can be infinitely divided up, will our arrow not always have to travel through one point before it can hit another point? So, obviously our arrow can never reach its target as it has an infinite number of destinations it needs to visit before it can ever arrive. One can achieve a similar outcome if one imagines that time is made up of tiny discrete moments. If an arrow occupies a particular space in one moment, how does it move to the adjoining space in the next moment? After all it cannot move within a moment. In either scenario, movement seems impossible. Zeno used argumentation like this to prove that it will be impossible for fleet-footed Achilles to overtake a slow-moving tortoise. Every time Achilles reaches the point where the tortoise was (X), it has moved just a little bit forward (X+1), and the same thing happens again when he catches it at that point (X+1): it has already moved on (X+1+0.5), and so on. Provided that both bodies stay in motion, it is theoretically impossible for Achilles to overtake the tortoise. The tortoise will always be that infinitesimally small bit ahead.

Such paradoxes can be refuted (presumably the easiest way would be to ask Zeno to stand in front of an archery target and ask him if he still believed that arrows could not fly through the air), but their cumulative effect is to make us deeply uncertain about what it is that we can truly say that we know. There is a political dimension to this. In archaic Greece, kings claimed a divine right to rule and dispense justice. However, if the Gods were different than we imagined or laws were just a series of customs, or morality was just a series of conventions, then why should we obey traditional rulers? It is no coincidence that the birth of philosophy coincided with a tremendous upheaval in political regimes. The sixth and the beginning of the fifth century was a period of coup and counter-coup as often fierce fighting divided elites. Philosophers were the apologists for regime change. For all its claims to be the work of outsiders, philosophy was intimately connected with the life of the city. Without an audience to play off and question him, Diogenes would just be a madman alone in a barrel. It is society that makes him a philosopher.

▶ Socrates and Plato

The group of thinkers that we have just discussed are conventionally called 'pre-Socratics'. Naturally, they did not call themselves this. Moreover, it is unlikely that they ever conceived of themselves as a homogenous group.

The fact that we choose such a label actually tells us less about the 'pre-Socratics' than it does about the importance that we place on Socrates (469–399 BC). Or rather, to be more correct, the importance that we place on the figure of Socrates as depicted by his most important disciple Plato (429–347 BC).

Socrates left no writings. Many of the stories about him are contradictory. Piecing together the 'real Socrates' is a difficult and thankless task. About his life, we know little for certain. He was an Athenian citizen, lived in Athens, and fought for her in a couple of important battles in the Peloponnesian War. He does not seem to have participated in politics, but he did serve a term as a member of the important Athenian Council that prepared the agendas for meetings of the Assembly. He was famous for his ugliness – with his snub-nose he was said to resemble more a satyr than a man. Although not rich, Socrates seems to have been relatively comfortable.

We are much better informed about his death. In 399 BC, he was put on trial for impiety and 'corrupting the young'. Socrates had certainly not endeared himself to many in the city. He delighted in exposing the ignorance of politicians, generals and philosophers with his questioning. However, the real motive behind the trial seems to be the fact that a number of Socrates' students had been very prominent in the short-lived pro-Spartan junta that ruled Athens following her defeat in the Peloponnesian War. The rule of this government had been particularly brutal, and following the restoration of democracy, the ringleaders were condemned. Socrates seems to have been tarred by association. When he was sentenced to death, nobody expected the sentence to be carried out. They expected him to go into exile. Perverse to the end, Socrates chose to drink the poison hemlock and died surrounded by his friends and students.

Most of the philosophic ideas that we associate with Socrates are really the product of Plato. In his *Dialogues*, Plato purports to report various conversations between Socrates and prominent individuals. Inevitably, Socrates always triumphs as these interlocutors tie themselves in knots as they attempt to answer Socrates' probing questions. Through Socrates, Plato teaches his readers as much about how to argue as he does about what to think. The 'Socratic method' of question and answer is still rightly revered today as a form of education.

Over the course of these conversations, many topics are covered. These include the nature of beauty, the immortality of the soul, the best form of government for the State, and the issue of whether virtue can be taught and, if so, how. A number of the conclusions reached in these Dialogues proved extraordinarily influential on later thinkers. Plato's supposed proof of the immortality of the soul would become particularly important, being taken up by a number of early Christian thinkers. Similarly, his idea of the Forms would have a profound effect on philosophic thinking. In Plato's theory, there existed for every object and quality an ideal type or version of which the types that existed in the world were just a pale imitation. We live in a world of poor reflections of an ultimate reality. For example, in our world chairs come in different sizes and shapes, they wear and break. In the world of the Forms, there is only one chair, perfect, unchanging and immortal. We recognize the chairs that exist in our world as 'chairs' despite the different versions they come in because our immortal souls once lived in the world of the Forms and can dimly recollect this ideal form of a chair. The aim of philosophy is to help us understand the 'true' form of the objects that surround us. In a potent image, Plato compared our existence to a prisoner who has spent his entire life living in a cave, chained up, staring at a wall with his back to the entrance of the cave. Behind the prisoner a roaring fire burns and an elaborate shadow puppet show plays out. The prisoner, not knowing anything else, mistakes the shadows for reality. The echoes he hears in the cave, he mistakes for the true sound that objects make. The role of the philosopher was to release us from our chains, get us to turn around, leave the cave, bypass the puppet show, and enter the light, the world of the true Forms. This is not necessarily a pleasant experience. It will be painful and frightening. The strong, true light blinds the eyes of those who dwell in the cave and they will initially want to return to the comfort of the world of the shadows. However, once their eyes adjust and they see things as they truly are, they will not to return to their cave existence. In fact, the opposite will apply – they will want to free the other prisoners in the cave and show them the real nature of the world. In this powerful metaphor, Plato establishes both a purpose and an ethical basis for the practice of philosophy.

▶ Aristotle

Plato used another metaphor, the metaphor of the butcher, to describe the role of the philosopher. Their aim should be to 'cut nature at the joint' and expose the constituent parts. Plato expressed the aim; Aristotle (384–322 BC) fulfilled it. No philosopher in the ancient world can match Aristotle for his ability to pull things apart and describe the resulting elements. This is a practice that informs all of his works. Whether the subject was an octopus, a tragic play or a system of government, each in turn was rigorously described, categorized and analysed.

There is an old joke about a student who complains to his teacher about the quality of his education. 'I wish I had a teacher like Aristotle,' he laments. To which comes the immediate reply, 'And I, a student like Alexander the Great'. The joke works because only a figure like Alexander can match a figure like Aristotle. Any other name and the riposte would lose its sting. It also highlights one of the great coincidences of history that the most famous warrior in antiquity had as his tutor the most famous mind in antiquity. Never has so much brawn met so much brain. Yes, despite their differences, the two have much in common.

Boundless ambition and a love of hard work are some of the aspects that they share. As we have seen, there was no shortage of clever men in antiquity, but none can rival Aristotle for the volume of work that he produced. Over 150 titles are known, of which approximately one fifth survives today. The volume is impressive, but so is the breadth. There is almost no area of philosophy that Aristotle did not touch.

A large amount of his writings are devoted to topics that we would classify today as 'scientific'. He is justly famous for his zoological writings, which represent the first attempt in the West to classify and describe all the various types of animals found in the environment. He was interested in all aspects of animal behaviour, from the way that animals moved to the way they ate and copulated. In addition to his zoological writings, Aristotle also wrote in the fields of medicine, embryology, mineralogy, botany and meteorology.

To assist him in his endeavours, Aristotle developed strict laws of argumentation. With Aristotle, we see the first treatises on logic. The systems of analysis and argumentation that he developed were then applied to a wide variety of fields. Through his various works he addressed questions of how people should behave (Nicomachean Ethics), the nature of existence (Metaphysics), how literature should be written (Poetics), how speeches should be structured (Rhetoric), and how cities should be governed (Politics). There was little that escaped his critical faculties.

This did not mean that Aristotle always arrived at the right answer. His views on the inferior capacities of women and their subordinate role in reproduction are infamous. Similarly scandalous are his ideas on slavery. His claim that some people have slavish natures and that the best thing for them is to be enslaved had unfortunate consequences. So influential were Aristotle's opinions that for centuries afterwards his words were quoted to justify the unjustifiable. Both those opposing the rights of women and the freeing of slaves were happy to cite Aristotle in support of their reactionary views.

▶ Philosophers of health

When Aristotle formulated his theories of the body, he was not working in isolation. From the sixth century BC onwards, numerous thinkers had turned their attention to the issue of how our bodies work, what are the functions of our organs, and what causes disease, and how it might be cured.

These fathers of Greek medicine were 'philosophers of health'. Like the pre-Socratic philosophers, they shared a suspicion towards ideas of divine causation. Rather than seeing disease as punishment from the gods or a by-product of magical curses, they sought explanation rooted in the physical world.

We see this in one of the earliest medical texts, 'On the Sacred Disease'. The so-called 'sacred disease' was that which we now call epilepsy. In antiquity, epilepsy was often regarded as a sign of divine possession, a by-product of the presence of Gods. In this treatise, the author debunks this theory, arguing that it is just a disease like any other, and if we were to call it 'sacred' then we would need to call all diseases 'sacred'.

Like philosophers, philosophers of health worked with large, over-arching theories such as the humoral theory of medicine. According to this theory, man's health is determined by four substances (humours): blood, yellow bile, black bile and phlegm. When these substances are in balance, then good health is achieved. Having them out of balance (either too much or too little) causes pain and disease. In humoral medicine, the job of the doctor is first to determine which humour is the cause of the disease and then to prescribe a regime that will restore balance to the body. Sometimes this balance can be restored by diet; sometimes stronger interventions are needed, such as bloodletting.

They were equally ambitious in seeking fame. By the sixth century BC, we see Greek physicians at the courts of a number of rulers, both Greek and foreign. Writers such Hippocrates (c. 460–370 BC) became a byword for medical excellence. So much so, that even after his death, works were still attributed to him to increase their cache. The oath that bears his name has become the definitive statement of medical ethics. The Romans also prized the opinion of Greek medical writers. The most famous of these, Galen (c. AD 129–216), became a trusted intimate of Marcus Aurelius.

Galen's writings would become the basis of western medicine for centuries. It is hard to overstate the size of his legacy. Its value is more debatable. Thanks to Galen, humoral medicine became the standard form of medicine. The esteem in which he was held stymied progress. People were too reluctant to accept that he was wrong. The lives lost due to inappropriate bloodletting is countless. In this, we see the danger of the classical legacy: sometimes we put the Ancients on too high a pedestal.

▶ Other traditions

Whenever modern philosophers are asked to name the world's greatest philosopher, the answer is almost always Aristotle. He is responsible for so much that is important in modern philosophy. His forms of argumentation, his rules of logic and his propositions in metaphysics all form the basis of much modern philosophic practice.

It is less clear that ancient students would have given Aristotle such a pre-eminent place in their discussion. Other teachers were equally or even more respected. Philosophers were famous for their rivalry and lack of respect for each other. The anti-social Diogenes reserved special scorn for Plato, whose lectures he routinely abused as a waste of time. According to one famous anecdote, when Plato once offered a definition of 'man' as 'a naked biped', Diogenes rushed into his lecture room with a plucked chicken, declaring, 'Behold, Plato's man'. Plato was forced to amend his definition to read 'a featherless biped with flat fingernails'. The story is almost certainly false, but it neatly captures the spirit of rivalry that existed between various philosophers.

For the curious mind, there were a number of different philosophic schools to choose from.

Two schools proved particularly important in Rome – the Stoics and Epicureans. Rather than just a set of beliefs, these schools offered a way of living that governed aspects such a dress, diet, career and exercise. It would prove a popular recipe, especially with members of the Roman elite. Indeed, even members of the imperial family found these philosophies attractive. One of the most significant texts for the study of stoicism is the *Meditations* by the second century AD emperor Marcus Aurelius (AD 121–180).

The Stoic school was founded in the third century BC in Athens by the philosopher Zeno of Citium (c. 334–c. 262 BC, not to be confused with Zeno of Elea whose paradoxes we discussed above). This group of philosophers takes their name from the colonnade (Gk. *Stoa*) in the marketplace in Athens from which Zeno held forth with his teachings.

Stoics are best known for their moral philosophy on how one should live one's life. However, it is important to remember that their philosophic enquiries were broad. There were Stoic opinions on cosmology, physics and logic. Indeed, the logic of one Stoic by the name of Chrysippus was regarded by many in antiquity as even more important than the logic of Aristotle.

The most famous ethical teachings of the Stoics relate to their belief that the best life was a virtuous one freed from passion. It was excessive emotion that, they argued, was the cause of so much unhappiness.

Through the application of reason and self-examination, it was possible to gain control of one's emotions and so avoid pain.

The Stoic notion of virtue centred on the qualities of wisdom, courage, justice and temperance. A life that followed these cardinal virtues was worth living. The problem came when circumstances and necessity would not allow you to live virtuously. This could be particularly a problem if you were a prominent Roman living under a despotic emperor. In such circumstances, Stoics were even prepared to countenance suicide. The most celebrated example of such a suicide was Seneca (c. 4 BC–AD 65), the Stoic philosopher and tutor of Nero, who was implicated in the opposition to the emperor and ordered to commit suicide. In true philosophic spirit, even as he died, Seneca could not resist teaching – instructing his friends to observe the pattern of his life, if they hoped to achieve virtue and fame.

Stoics have a slightly undeserved modern reputation for austerity and severity. However, this is nothing compared to the modern misrepresentation of their great philosophic rivals, the Epicureans. Never has a quote been so misunderstood as the Epicurean maxim that, 'we say that pleasure is the beginning and end of living happily'. Opponents, such as early Christians, were only too happy to transform this maxim into a prescription for wild debauchery and an excessive dedication to the delights of the table. Nothing could be further from the truth. Epicureans were a serious philosophic school whose teachings not only included discussions of ways of living, but also theology, epistemology, logic and physics. They were committed to the notion of a rational universe whose basic building blocks were uncuttable particles of matter ('atoms').

As we have seen already, philosophy was largely about creating a lifestyle that was opposed to the general run of things. Epicureans were no different. To portray them as the 'party boys' of the philosophic world does them a great disservice. The secluded 'garden' in Athens to which Epicurus (341–270 BC) and his students retreated was no den of hedonism. When Epicureans talk about pleasure, they mean a very specific form of pleasure. Believing that much pain came from unsatisfied desire and irrational fears, they eschewed pleasures that were transitory or unattainable. The goal was to achieve tranquillity – freedom from disturbance. Friendship and the quiet life were their desired goals. Not even death worried the Epicureans. It was nothing to be feared. After all, we do not worry about the time before we came into being, so why should we worry about the time after we have passed away? When we exist, death is not present, and when death is present, we do not exist. With its focus on simple meaningful pleasures, Epicureanism was a comforting philosophy that found many adherents. One can see why the Christians hated it.

This 100 ideas section gives ways you can explore the subject in more depth. It's much more than the usual reading list.

100 IDEAS

20 Greek sites to visit

1. Acropolis, Athens, Greece
2. Delphi, Greece
3. Ephesus, Turkey
4. Knossos, Crete, Greece
5. Pergamum, Turkey
6. Olympia, Greece
7. Temple of Apollo Epicurus, Bassae, Greece
8. Ancient Corinth, Greece
9. The Agora, Athens, Greece
10. Mycenae, Greece

11. Temple of Poseidon at Sounion, Greece

12. Akrotiri, Santorini, Greece

13. Cyrene, Libya

14. Agrigento (Acragas), Sicily

15. Temple of Aphaia, Aigina, Greece

16. Poseidonia (Paestum), Italy

17. Epidaurus, Greece

18. Sanctuary of Artemis, Brauron, Greece

19. Tiryns, Greece

20. Amphiareion, Oropos, Greece

20 Roman sites to visit

1. The Flavian Amphitheatre ('The Colosseum'), Rome, Italy

2. The Forum, Rome, Italy

3. Pompeii, Italy

4. Leptis Magna, Libya

5. Trajan's Column, Rome, Italy

6. Hadrian's Villa, Tivoli, Italy

7. Pont du Gard, France

8. Ara Pacis, Rome, Italy

9. Herculaneum, Italy

10. Baalbeck, Lebanon

11. Diocletian's Palace, Split, Croatia

12. Hadrian's Wall, UK

13. Roman Baths, Bath, UK

14. Fishbourne Roman Palace, UK

15. Maison Carrée, Nîmes, France

16. Sperlonga Cave and Museum, Italy

17. Villa Jovis, Capri, Italy

18. Baths of Caracalla, Rome, Italy

19. Pantheon, Rome, Italy

20. Jerash, Jordan

10 Greek objects to see

1. Parthenon Marbles, British Museum, London, UK

2. Pergamum Altar, Berlin, Germany

3. Mask of Agamemnon, National Archaeological Museum, Athens, Greece

4. Kritios Boy, Acropolis Museum, Athens, Greece

5. Nike of Samothrace, Louvre, Paris, France

6. Venus de Milo, Louvre, Paris, France

7. Antikythera Mechanism, National Archaeological Museum, Athens, Greece

8. François Vase, National Archaeological Museum, Florence, Italy

9. Exekias' Vatican Amphora, Vatican City

10. Motya Charioteer, Villa Whitaker, Mozia, Italy

10 Roman objects to see

1. Augustus of Prima Porta statue, Vatican City

2. Laocoön and His Sons, Museo Pio-Clementino, Vatican City

3. Gemma Augustea, Kunsthistorisches Museum, Vienna, Austria

4. Colossus of Constantine, Capitoline Museum, Rome, Italy

5. Portland Vase, British Museum, London, UK

6. Pan and Goat statue, National Archaeological Museum, Naples, Italy

7. Boscoreale Treasure, Louvre, Paris, France

8. The Warren Cup, British Museum, London, UK

9. Bust of Pompey the Great, Ny Carlsberg Glyptotek, Copenhagen, Denmark

10. Fish Mosaic, National Archaeological Museum, Naples, Italy

10 Latin phrases to know

1. Audentis fortuna iuvat ('Fortune favours the brave', Vergil, *Aeneid* 10.284)

2. Carpe diem ('Seize the day', Horace, *Odes* I.11.8)

3. Veni, Vidi, Vici ('I came, I saw, I conquered', Suetonius, *Life of Julius Caesar* 37)

4. Quis custodiet ipsos custodes? ('Who watches the watchmen?', Juvenal, *Satires* 6.347-8)

5. Iacta alea est ('The die is cast', Suetonius, *Life of Julius Caesar* 32)

6. Cuiusvis hominis est errare, nullius nisi insipientis in errore perseverare ('Any man can make a mistake; only a fool keeps making the same one', Cicero, *Philippics* 12.2.5)

7. Timeo Danaos et dona ferentes ('I fear the Greeks, even those bearing gifts', Vergil, *Aeneid* 2.49)

8. Ars longa, vita brevis ('Art is long, but life is short', a Latin translation of Hippocrates' maxim Ὁ βίος βραχύς, ἡ δὲ τέχνη μακρή')

9. Ave, Caesar, morituri te salutant ('Hail, Caesar, those about to die salute you', Suetonius, *Life of Claudius* 21.6)

10. 'Cui bono' ('Who does this benefit?' Cicero, *Pro Roscio Amerino* 84)

10 Works of Latin literature to read

1. Vergil, *Aeneid*

2. Ovid, *Metamorphoses*

3. Tacitus, *Annals*

4. Petronius, *Satyrica*

5. Apuleius, *Golden Ass*

6. Catullus, *Poems*

7. Suetonius, *Lives of the Caesars*

8. Seneca, *Letters*

9. Horace, *Odes*

10. Martial, *Epigrams*

10 Works of Greek literature to read

1. Homer, *Iliad*
2. Plutarch, *Lives of Famous Greeks and Romans*
3. Herodotus, *Histories*
4. Aeschylus, *Agamemnon*
5. Aristophanes, *Lysistrata*
6. Sophocles, *Oedipus Rex*
7. Euripides, *Trojan Women*
8. Plato, *Symposium*
9. Sappho, *Poems*
10. Thucydides, *History of the Peloponnesian War*

10 Films about the Ancient World

1. *Ben Hur* (1959, dir. Wyler)
2. *Spartacus* (1960, dir. Kubrick)
3. *Sign of the Cross* (1932, dir. DeMille)
4. *Quo Vadis* (1951, dir. LeRoy)
5. *300* (2006, dir. Snyder)
6. *Fall of the Roman Empire* (1964, dir. Mann)
7. *Cleopatra* (1963, dir. Mankiewicz)
8. *Hercules* (1958, dir. Francisci)
9. *Alexander* (2004, dir. Stone)
10. *Fellini Satyricon* (1969, dir. Fellini)

Further reading

General reference works

Oxford Classical Dictionary, edited by Hornblower, S., Spawforth, A. and Eidinow, E., 4th edition, Oxford: Oxford University Press

Barrington Atlas of the Greek and Roman World, edited by Talbert, R. J. A., Princeton: Princeton University Press

Specialist works

Beard, M. (2007) *The Roman Triumph*. Cambridge, Mass.: Belknap Press of Harvard University Press

Cartledge, P. A. (1993) *The Greeks: A Portrait of Self and Others*. Oxford: Oxford University Press

Galinksy, Karl (1996) *Augustan Culture: An interpretive introduction*. Princeton: Princeton University Press

Goodman, M. (2002) *The Roman World, 44 BC–AD 180*. Routledge History of the Ancient World. London: Taylor and Francis

Green, P. (1990) *Alexander to Actium: The Historical Evolution of the Hellenistic Age*. Berkeley and Los Angeles: University of California Press

Osborne, R. (2009) *Greece in the Making, 1200–479 BC*. Routledge History of the Ancient World. London: Taylor and Francis

Rhodes, P. J. (2010) *A History of the Classical Greek World, 478–323 BC*. 2nd edition. Blackwell History of the Ancient World. Chichester: Wiley-Blackwell

Woodford, S. (2004) *The Art of Greece and Rome*. Cambridge: Cambridge University Press

Index